J. Robert Hutchinson, K. Viresalingam

Fortune's Wheel

A Tale of Hindu domestic Life

J. Robert Hutchinson, K. Viresalingam

Fortune's Wheel
A Tale of Hindu domestic Life

ISBN/EAN: 9783337076849

Printed in Europe, USA, Canada, Australia, Japan

Cover: Foto ©ninafisch / pixelio.de

More available books at **www.hansebooks.com**

FORTUNE'S WHEEL.

A Tale of Hindu Domestic Life.

BY

K. VIRESALINGAM, PANDIT.

TRANSLATED BY
J. ROBERT HUTCHINSON.

With a Preface by
GENERAL MACDONALD,
LATE DIRECTOR OF PUBLIC INSTRUCTION, MADRAS PRESIDENCY, INDIA.

LONDON:
ELLIOT STOCK, 62, PATERNOSTER ROW, E.C.
1887.

TRANSLATOR'S PREFACE.

That stronghold of Hinduism, the native home, has never yet been carried. It stands impregnable within rugged walls of caste prejudice and ancestral usage. The barriers it opposes to the inquisitive outsider— barriers of race, caste, and religion—are barriers of steel ; slowly corroding now, it is true, but still effectually strong to prevent curious intrusion. In this citadel of the Hindu people hangs the key to their hearts and minds and lives ; and of this key the excluded foreigner can never hope to possess himself. Our knowledge of the domestic economy and social life of the Hindu family must, under existing circumstances, come from within the home itself.

Apart from its intense interest as a work of fiction, the following tale (written by a high-caste Hindu) is, in this respect, of special value. It is the 'open sesame' before which the door of the Hindu abode flies open, revealing the complete inner life of a representative Hindu family—their home, dress, food, worship, modes of thought and speech, joys and sorrows, loves and hates, hopes and fears ; their simple, unquestioning piety, so strangely blended with rank superstition ; the secluded quiet of their existence ; their calm stoicism and unmurmuring resignation to the decrees of fate. In a word, the tale unlocks the street-door, introduces the reader to the inmates, shows him over the house, and makes him feel quite at home notwithstanding the bewildering strangeness of his surroundings.

The numerous live social questions of the day in India have their origin in this seclusion of all domestic life within four walls. Nor does the writer ignore this important fact. The subject position of women, and their education; the inhuman treatment and wretched condition of widows; the quackeries of native charlatans, the consequent sufferings of the sick, and the opening thus presented for trained physicians of both sexes; child-marriage, with all its heartless intrigue and unnatural horrors; the remarriage of unfortunate child-widows—these and many kindred topics are treated powerfully and with enlightened good sense. While to crown all, the story into which these topics are woven is of intense interest and thoroughly Hindu.

INTRODUCTION.

COMPLAINTS are sometimes made that the educated natives of India have not done as much as they ought for the improvement of their vernacular literature. The Pandits, it is said, must be expected to work in their old groove, but something new ought to be produced by men who have been brought in contact with the literature of Europe, and have had the advantage of studying models unknown to their countrymen. Every effort to remove this reproach must be viewed with interest, or at least with indulgence. Kandukuri Viresalingam, Telugu Pandit of the Government College at Rajahmundry, who has had the advantage of receiving some English education, some years ago conceived the idea of translating the 'Vicar of Wakefield' into Telugu, but eventually decided on writing a tale of Hindu domestic life, in which the scene is laid in his own district, and little or nothing is borrowed from Goldsmith beyond the general idea of a family in easy circumstances reduced to poverty. Himself an ardent reformer, he has made his story a vehicle for exposing the evils of child-marriage and the miserable condition of Hindu widows. He shows us how large a part a belief in astrology, omens, fortune-telling, magic and witchcraft plays in Hindu life. He takes us into Rukmini's sick-room and exhibits the absurdity of the treatment to which she is subjected by a celebrated native practitioner. The tricks of religious impostors are satirized

INTRODUCTION.

in the episodes of the roguish Býragi, who professes to be an alchemist, and of the sanctimonious Yogi, who is in league with a gang of robbers. The Guru Sri Chidananda Sankarabharati-swami exemplifies the rapacity and licentiousness of the class of spiritual teachers of whom he is a type.

The English reader must not expect to find any traces of the delicate delineation of character and quiet humour which give such a charm to Goldsmith's inimitable idyl. The main value of the book lies in its minute descriptions of that domestic life which is so imperfectly known to Europeans. We sit down in the choultry on the banks of the Godavery and hear the flatteries addressed to the rich man of the village by his obsequious friends. We listen to the gossip of the women, who have come down to draw water and perform their ablutions. We follow Rajasekhara into his house; we see his wife grinding sandal-wood, and his niece cooking the midday meal. We observe how he is sponged on by distant relatives and perfect strangers. We hear him importuned for additional subscriptions for the support of the worship of Janardana-swami, who, like the gods of a good many other shrines, has seven putties of land, of which five go to the dancing-women and two to the priests. We see the silent disapproval with which Rajasekhara's attempts to educate his daughter are viewed at a period when reading and writing were considered accomplishments suited only to courtesans. We watch him and his boy listening to the poor Sastri, who comes in to expound the Mahabhárata. We see Rajasekhara gradually sinking into poverty, and at last compelled to mortgage his house and set out with his family on a pilgrimage to Benares. He never, however, gets further than Peddapuram, and after some adventures returns a wiser man to his old home.

In the course of the narrative we have some pleasing descriptions of local scenery. We go into the temples and mingle with the crowds during the celebration of various religious festivals. We are introduced to the Courts of two Rajahs. We hear of some rather improbable adventures with tigers. The incidents are perhaps scarcely of a character to prove very attractive to the ordinary novel-reader, and a less faithful translation might have given the book a better chance of success in the circulating library, but not success of a desirable kind.

Rajasekhara set out on his pilgrimage in 1618-1619. At this period the white strangers were not far off, for they had already commenced trading at Masulipatam and Nizampatam; but there are no references to them in the story, nor do we come across a single Mussulman, although Ramamurti does ask the astrologer how long the country is to remain under the yoke of the foreigner.

During the two centuries and a half which have elapsed since the period to which the tale relates, the face of the country has undergone great changes. At Dhavalesvaram, where the story opens, the magnificent stream of the Godavery is now spanned by the great anicut constructed by Sir Arthur Cotton, and the district is covered with a network of canals, which fertilize the fields and carry boatloads of travellers with an ease undreamt of in the days of Rajasekhara. Broad roads run through tracts which were once covered with jungle, and, since the establishment of Sir William Robinson's police, such highway robberies as that described by the author have ceased to be common. English education is slowly undermining the ancient faith. But the external aspect of Hindu society changes very slowly. The life described in the story is the life of the present day. The author has drawn most of his pictures from the scenes among which he is living. It is this realism which gives the book whatever merit it possesses.

Owing to the excellence of the Telugu in which it is written, and the insight which it gives us into native manners, the original story may be perused with advantage by young civilians, military officers, missionaries, and other persons whose duties require them to study the language. A translation of this Telugu novel, by the Rev. J. R. Hutchinson, has recently appeared in the pages of the *Madras Christian College Magazine*, and is now presented in a more permanent form to the English public.

It is to be hoped that the reception accorded to his first work may be of such a character as to encourage him to persevere in his efforts. Missionaries have done a great deal to bring India closer to England, but there is still much to be achieved, and a friendly welcome should await every fresh labourer in this wide field of usefulness.

R. M. MACDONALD.

FORTUNE'S WHEEL.

CHAPTER I.

Dhavalagiri—Description of the Temple—Rajasekhara sitting in the Rest-house on the Bank of the Godaveri at Early Morning—The Flatteries of the Astrologer and others who resort there—All go together to the Feet of Rama to see the *Byragi*.

NEAR Sri Nassakatryambaka, somewhere in the far East, the Godaveri river has her birth in a lofty mountain. Sparkling with the scintillations of her rings and wristlets, she meanders along the valleys on the slopes of Bhubhrudvara, her birthplace, and, tarrying a little, glides from thence gently onward, filling the eyes of all beholders with delight. Then flaunting saucily with sweet though indistinct utterances, she runs swift as an arrow, and, reaching the mighty trees, flouts the parent roots to dally with their younger offspring. Again, she plays hide-and-seek among the bulrushes; then escapes and journeys through Vidarbha and adjacent territories, refreshing all, whether young or old, and furnishing so abundant a supply of water for drinking and bathing that the fault is theirs alone who, coming that way, refuse to take it. She vivifies and renders fruitful the crops and fruit-trees in every place where she sets her foot; adorns the whole land on either bank, as far as her coolness extends, with soft green grass; provides food for vast herds of cattle; welcomes to her embrace the Varada, Manjira, Pinnaganga, and other rivers, which hear her coming from afar and rush by many roads to meet her, bearing as tribute fruits of the desert and peacock plumes; views from afar that white mountain in the neighbourhood of Rajahmundry which has attained celebrity as the richest gem of the Telugu country, and, betraying her depth the more as she comes on and on seeking her husband, rushes melodiously along its base to pay her respects to *Janardana-swami** who dwells upon the summit, and immediately stretching out from thence her hands (in the form of two branches), gains the coveted boon and coyly joins her lord.

This mountain is not of great height; but, being composed of white mica rock, is a veritable wonder to behold. It is on account of these same rocks that it bears the name Dhavalagiri, or White Mountain. On the south side are built stairs of black stone from the base straight up to the brow of the hill. On either side of these extend up the slope, in a line that delights the eye, the dwellings of priests and other devotees of Vishnu. These stairs ascended, there appears upon the summit a small but beautiful temple of black stone. Around this on three sides extends a wall of about the height of a man. On the north side, however, instead of the wall the horn of the mountain itself shoots upward, and affording the walls a shelter at its base, towers above them and peeps over the dome of the temple itself. Within this enclosure, to the north, is a small cave. The ancients say that when of old the princes of the house of Pandu† lived as hermits, they sat here and did penance. There was in it at the time of our story a small stone image.

* An epithet of Vishnu. Swami is a general term for objects of worship.

† The princes of the house of Pandu. Pandu was the half-brother of Dhritarashtra. Having incurred a curse in consequence of killing a stag, he retired to the Himalayas, where he died. Here he had sons born to him by his wives, the progeny of deities—Yudhishthira, Bhima, Arjuna, Nakula, and Sahadeva.

On the feast-days of this god, which throughout the remainder of the year moulders without offering or adoration, the priest brings it out, cleans it with tamarind-water, and places a small lighted lamp in the divine presence. Then, standing in the entrance of the cave, he takes a penny a head from the crowds of people who come on pilgrimage from the surrounding hamlets, goes within and worships the god, and dismisses them with the assurance that their ancestors have been blessed.* No sooner do the half-dozen nuptial days of *Janardana-swami* come to an end than the priests place him as usual among the ropes of his car, and station the little god as sentry over him. This minor deity, though possessing neither salary nor means of daily subsistence, moves not a foot, but steadfastly stands guard day and night; while the priests, through faith in him, live a life free from anxiety or necessity for entering the cave again until next year this rope business comes round once more. But though irreligious man thus fail to wait upon the god, the little four-footed beasts that guard the mountain pay their pious homage constantly to the deity; and until men return on feast-days and commit so great a sin as to drive them out, make their very bed at night before the god on the bare floor of the cave.

Within the enclosure, on the eastern side, there stands before *Janardana-swami* a lofty standard. The tiny bells upon its top for ever sway back and forth in the breeze, and delight the ear with their sweet music. At the base of the shaft, facing the god with joined hands, stands an image of Anjaneya.† To the north of this

---

* The Hindus practise ancestor-worship. They believe that such worship as that mentioned above accelerates the progress of the soul to heaven. One of their poets thus satirizes the practice:

'If offerings of food can satisfy
Hungry departed spirits, why supply
The man who goes a journey, with provisions?
His friends at home can feed him with oblations.'

† The chief of the deified monkeys, and an ally and spy of Rama.

stone image and the standard is a nuptial porch. On the wedding-days of the god they seat the processional images in this porch, and conduct the whole marriage ceremony with the utmost pomp.*

In each fortnight of the month,† on the night of the eleventh day, occurs the praise-service of Vishnu. The Vaishnavas assume their rosaries of *tulasi* beads,‡ plaster on the twelve perpendicular marks,§ and, fingering their lutes to the braying of cymbals and drums and shouting with all their might the names of their tutelary deity—'O Butter Thief!' 'O Enjoyer of the Shepherdesses!' 'O Lover of Radhika!' 'O Shepherd Boy!' ‖ sing the exploits of Krishna, and chew pepper-corns and lumps of sugar between whiles to relieve their hoarse throats. With wagging heads the devotees put forth all their strength and play so hard that frequently the drums and cymbals are broken. It often happens, too, that one or two of the more pious fall into a trance by divine inspiration, and lean back upon the pillars behind for several minutes at a time, insensible. To foreigners who do not at all understand this sort of devotion, their actions at such times seem like the antics of madmen; but as for the people who come to see the show—the more the devotees yell with distorted features, the greater saints they consider them.

If anyone take the trouble to climb the mountain

---

* The marriage of the principal Hindu deities is celebrated once a year. Idols are of two classes—processional, or movable, and fixed images. The image of Anjaneya is an example of the latter.

† Each lunar month has two *pakshas*, or periods of two weeks. The first is called the *sukla* or light, the second the *krishna* or dark, fortnight.

‡ The sacred basil (*ocymum sanctum*), a plant worshipped by the Hindus.

§ The twelve perpendicular marks worn by Vaishnavas. Three each are drawn with wet ashes of cow-dung upon the forehead, shoulders, and breast.

‖ These names are twenty-four in number, and are drawn from the chief exploits of that jolly god, Krishna, when incarnate. Radhika was his aunt, and a favourite mistress during his residence among the cowherds. She was also wife of Ayana Ghosha, the Nameless.

at mid-day and direct his gaze to the four quarters of the heavens, he will behold a veritable feast for the eyes. Along the mountain-side the goats, erect upon their hind-legs, nibble the foliage of the bushes, while their vari-coloured kids frolic nimbly before them. To the east and south, among a seeming heap of thatched houses, towers aloft an occasional tiled roof, as in derision of its meaner neighbours. To the north the field-watchers shout 'Ko! Ko!' from their elevated perches, and whirl their rattles to frighten away the numerous flocks of birds. Of these, many varieties rise from the neighbouring groves into the sky, uttering their sweet calls, and when opportunity affords break off the milky heads of unripe grain and light again upon the branches of the trees to eat. Here, too, the herds of cattle in the meadows crop the blades of grass between whiles, or wholly stop grazing and with their calves stand listening, their ears erect, necks outstretched, and hearts melting at the songs of the shepherd boys who sing to the melodious accompaniment of the pipe in the shade of the trees. On the west the rays of the sun, falling upon the clear waters of the parent Godaveri, produce diamond-glintings in all directions; while many varieties of aquatic birds bob up and down upon the surface like puff-balls as they skim along the eddies catching fish.

On the bank of the Godaveri, near the base of this mountain, the Feet of Rama have come to light neatly imprinted in a black stone slab. Everyone believes these to be the prints of the very feet that trod the path near this mountain, when of old Sri Rama went to the hermitage with Sita and Lakshmana. Pilgrims, desirous of visiting the Feet of Rama, journey hither even from distant countries. Here, near Rama's shrine, they bathe in Mother Godaveri, climb the mountain and offer fruit and alms to *Janardana-swami* according to their several ability, or if they have the means, even make a feast to the god, and go their way again.

Since they have made this a meritorious shrine, all, without difference of creed or caste, receive the sour rice, rice and curd, and other oblations offered to the god, and apply them to their eyes and eat them on the spot; and as it is a misdemeanour to wash off what sticks to the hands, they paint the pillars and walls of the temple with their palms as high as they can reach, and then polish the backs of their hands and their cloths with what still remains.

For a short distance on the south and east of the mountain extends a village. Formerly this village bore the name of the hill itself; but at present they call it Dhavalesvaram. Just where the steps leave the hill, on the lower side of the high-road, stands the Temple of Sri Agastesvara-swami. The local legend says that of old Agastyu crushed the pride of the Vindhya Mountains, and, proceeding south, established this deity here.* Between the temple and the hill there extends from east to west, as far as the Godaveri, a broad highway. At the extremity of this street steps of black stone are built down to the water's edge; and near the steps, to the east of the road, is a building called a rest-house. It was originally intended for foreign Brahmans and other travellers to pass the night in; but finally came to be used only as a place of idle resort for the leading men of the village, who were in the habit of gathering there daily at morning and evening to pass the time in gossip.

The sun on rising one morning decorated himself as usual with his rouge *bottu*,† and gilded the tree-tops until he made them gleam as though they had blossomed into golden water. The birds with loud cries were leaving their nests, and flying off in all directions in quest of food. The shepherd boy (his lunch tied up in

---

* Agastyu is a celebrated personage in Hindu legend. He is fabled to have razed the Vindhya Mountains, and to have drunk the ocean dry.

† A distinctive caste-mark placed upon the forehead by the Hindus after bathing.

a bundle) was driving his cattle to the green meadows; while behind, the girls, baskets in hand, raced one another shouting, 'The white cow's dung is mine!' or 'The dun buffalo's dung is mine!' The farmers with goad on shoulder were driving their ploughs respectively afield, when a stout, middle-aged man, wearing his sacred thread after the manner of a necklace and carrying a brass drinking-vessel in his left hand, came wading to the bank after having washed his feet and hands in the Godaveri. Rinsing his mouth and ejecting the water, he arranged his sacred cord according to custom on the left shoulder, and came and sat down in the rest-house upon the bank. Here he proceeded to clean his teeth with a bit of crabstick which he had brought along in his drinking-cup when he came. His age was about forty. Had it not been for the small-pox pits upon it, there need have been no hesitation in pronouncing his face handsome. As it was, it was not at all unworthy of the blatant flatteries of those prophets who constantly visited him. In stature he was somewhat short and corpulent. His forehead was broad, leading beholders to think him a *pandit*.* He had on at the time a cloth of a watery-reddish tint. A laced cloth, newly washed, wound loosely about his head and hung down a little way behind. Except a small pair of diamond earrings in his ears, a gold ring in the form of a tuft of *darbha* grass which, on the ring-finger of his right hand, testified to the fact that he was a strict formalist,† and two silver rings on the forefinger, there were no ornaments whatever about his person. His name was Rajasekhara. By the time he had performed his facial ablutions a number of the inhabitants of the village came up. Saluting these as became their respective rank, he motioned them with his hand to be seated. Expressing their thanks profusely and begging

---

* A man of education.
† The *darbha* (*Poa cynosuroides*) is a sacred grass used in worshipg Brahmans who are strict in the observance of the ritual wear a gold rin. in the form of a tuft of this grass.

him to sit down first, they crowded the rest-house full.

'Astrologer,' said Rajasekhara, opening the conversation, 'you have entirely ceased visiting me of late. I suppose everybody is quite well at your house?'

'Thank you, thank you,' replied the astrologer; 'by your honour's favour we are all quite well. What can such people as we lack while your honour (a very jewel of the Lord!) is in the village? You are capable of protecting any number of families and supplying them with food and clothing. It is simply through our good fortune and the merit of our former existence,* that such benefactors as your honour deign to favour our village with their presence.' Then, turning to Rama-sastri, 'Of course it isn't the proper thing for me to praise him to his face; but, you must understand, Rajasekhara is simply divine.'

Rama-sastri signified his assent to this remark by a low laugh. 'Is there,' said he, 'any doubt of that? Is it necessary that you tell me this? It is only because he is in the place that we are able to remain. Otherwise, wouldn't it have been necessary long before this for us to leave house and home and get off to foreign lands? Since his honour's father settled here this has been something like a village; but before that it had neither "a local habitation nor a name."'

Thus whenever a good opportunity offered, he mixed in a few of his own praises as a spice to those of the astrologer, and that, too, without any attempt at hiding his learning.

'Astrologer,' said Rajasekhara, inwardly well pleased, but adroitly concealing his real feelings, 'I heard the other day that signs of possession had shown themselves in your—second daughter, I think? Is she any better?'

At this inquiry the astrologer's face betrayed con-

---

* Hinduism teaches that all good or bad fortune in this life is the ruit of the merit or demerit of actions performed in a previous existence.

siderable anxiety. After a moment's reflection he shook his head, and replied: 'I am having Josyula Kamavadhanulu exorcise her;* but so far it has had no effect whatever. According to her horoscope, too, the influence of Saturn is just now adverse to her. So, to see what that will do, I'm having my younger brother offer prayer to the nine planets.† But not satisfied with that even, I have myself been pursuing Kamavadhanulu, and importuning him to undertake the repetition of the *mantra* to Hanuman the Five-Faced,‡ and to perform a more efficacious exorcism, telling him that if anything is needed for the success of the rite, I'll give a few rupees, even though I have to catch some Rajasekhara or other, and carry him off *nolens volens* to do it. This is the only reason I have for not calling of late; otherwise, would I not have managed to visit you by some means or other?'

'Sastri,' replied Rajasekhara, 'you need not hesitate so far as the rupees are concerned. I'll give the whole four if necessary. And even if it takes another four you must look out for a good doctor. In our village Kamavadhanulu——' and glancing up at the sky he fell to reflecting on something or other. The astrologer's flattery was never lost upon Rajasekhara. It never took hold in vain, being always sure to bring more or less of a return in the shape of hard cash.

Neither in Dhavalesvaram nor in the surrounding villages was there another astrologer. People were or ever coming to his house to ask him to fix an hour for a journey, or to ascertain what time was unlucky, or what day was best for dividing and putting on a new cloth; what month was favourable for commencing the building of a new house, or what day of the week

---

* By applying ashes of cowdung, held sacred by the Hindus.

† The five major planets, the sun and moon, and *Rahu* and *Ketu* (the moon's ascending and descending nodes), are the nine *grahas* or heavenly bodies that appear to move. Each is supposed to have good or evil influences.

‡ Hanuman, the monkey-god, an ally and spy of Rama. His *mantra* (incantation) must be repeated one hundred thousand times.

propitious for having a shave; to beg him to determine the period for a wedding, or name the star at the occurrence of puberty. If they wished to know how long the defilement must continue when distant relatives died; if they desired to ascertain how long it was necessary to leave the house when anyone departed this life under an evil star; if they wished to learn what propitiatory rite was proper when a child was born in the fourth and similar lunar mansions—it was indispensable that they consult the astrologer. No matter what farmer's cattle strayed; no matter in whose house any article was missing; he would come without fail and consult the astrologer. On all such occasions as these he would spread sand on the ground in the street porch, write certain talismanic letters and numbers in it with the straw of a broom, look up for a moment as in deep reflection, and then dismiss the questioner with the assurance that so and so had happened, or that the affair would occur in such and such a manner. He also prognosticated the results of the fall of lizards and other reptiles, and by auguries foretold the time when an addition might be expected to the family. In short, in all the villages of that vicinity no event, whether auspicious or inauspicious, came off without the advice of the astrologer. His forecasts most frequently turned out to be sheer falsehood; but since now and then some things came true by mere coincidence, the people believed his word to be infallible.

One of the number then in the rest-house observing quietly that '*byragis** were adepts at witchcraft,' Rajasekhara turned to the astrologer and remarked: 'By the way, as soon as you mentioned *byragis* it occurred to me that I heard a report that some *byragi* or other had come to this place some ten days ago. Shouldn't you show the child to him? The medicinal roots and empirics of the ascetics are well known to these Gosains.† No matter how incurable the disease may

---

* Religious mendicants—*fakirs*.

† Secular monks or *fakirs*, who never marry, and who live in monasteries.

be, they rid you of it in a trice.' No sooner had he uttered these words than the whole rest-house was filled with cries of 'Good!' 'True!' 'He should certainly do as you say!' Let only a speaker be rich—even the most senseless utterance is sure to be counted worthy of applause. So Rajasekhara, made bold by these words, lauded the *byragi* to the skies, even though he himself had never seen him.

The astrologer dissembled on his features a pleasure which he did not feel at heart, and smiled a bland smile. 'At your honour's mere word,' said he, joining his hands with an appearance of humility and fixing his eyes on Rajasekhara's face; 'at your honour's mere word our little one's trouble is gone. It is certainly through her good luck alone that this advice emanated from my lord's countenance. In accordance with your honour's kind permission I will proceed at once to the *byragi*,' and he rose as though about to go. No sooner did Rajasekhara's opinion become somewhat generally known, than the whole assembly was overwhelmed in praises of the *byragi*. He was, they asserted, a most magnanimous man; an eminent magician; one who subsisted on air and did penance in the burning heat of summer in the midst of five fires. When a great man votes another a good fellow, who will rise in opposition? what tongue will grope in search of flatteries?

Just then Rajasekhara looked towards the street and remarked: 'Some women have come for water, and seeing us here have modestly retreated a few steps and stand looking aimlessly at one another. Come, let us all go and see the *byragi*.'

At this signal all arose, and proceeded together up the street in the direction of the Feet of Rama.

CHAPTER II.

Rajasekhara's daughter, Rukmini, comes to bathe—Description of the River-bank—Conversation between Rukmini and the Astrologer's Wife—The Gossip of the Maids and Matrons who come for Water—A *Panchanya* Brahmin comes and repeats Mantras—Rukmini bathes and goes Home.

WHEN Rajasekhara and the group of townsfolk had proceeded half a dozen steps on their way, a lovely girl, gathering her mantle deftly about her, and hanging her head to conceal a face on whose features modesty and shyness vied with each other, came straight down the steps with pretty graceful movement. The silver anklets upon her feet tinkled in unison with the music of her toe-rings; while the glittering silver belt about her waist and the golden and jet bracelets upon her wrists were reflected in picturesque hues by the copper cup that glinted in her right hand. Placing this cup at the water's edge, she removed a lump of saffron stuck on its rim and rubbed a little upon her body, laid a tiny packet of rouge she had brought wrapped up in a leaf on a stone for washing clothes, and waded knee-deep into the stream. She was Rajasekhara's eldest daughter, Rukmini. Ah me! The eyes so blessed as actually to gaze upon her beauty were eyes indeed! At that time among all the fair daughters of Ind the women of the Telugu land were unsurpassed in outline, grace, and blandishments. Among these, again, the women of the Brahman caste were by far the most debonair. But at the mere recollection of Rukmini's form all must hesitate to assert that these fair ones were in the least degree beautiful. In truth, I know not how to describe her beauty; for if the choicest of those who were confessedly handsome were selected and placed beside her, she would certainly prove them but ugly wenches. And it is an insult, I ween, to the majesty of her prettiness for me, unworthy in any sense to be compared with Kalidas and those other poets of old who possessed so divine an afflatus, to presume to paint her lofty beauty in a tongue destitute of phrases fitted to express it, and without the ability to depict it even as faithfully as existing phrases permit. Yet when a worthy object is found, it should not be abandoned without at least an attempt at description. And so I had thought, by comparing the symmetry of her limbs with some natural object, to suggest it, in a slight degree at least, to the imagination of the readers of this book; but again, when I consider her parts, I am ashamed even to utter that object's name. In a word, all who beheld her considered that even the Four-faced Creator himself could not fail to nod his approval of her form (a literal freak of Nature!) and praise his own creative skill. As regards her complexion, gold had no colour in the world when compared with it. Granting a bow to be black, it may be said that her eyebrows resembled it in a slight degree. Merely to see her eyes was to declare that Venus dwelt therein. But, had you examined the lineaments of her face closely, they would have indicated slightly that some fixed grief occupied the throne of her heart. That grief was not without cause; some months before, her husband, unfaithful, had clandestinely gone off to foreign parts.

She was now fourteen years old, and, like fragrance joined to gold,* already young womanhood lifted its head and added lustre to the elegance of her person. The white mantle, too, that she now had wrapped about her, gave a sort of grace, as blistered alum to gold. What does not become beautiful when worn by the fair? She also wore a jewel in her nose, gold ear-rings set with sapphires, finger-rings, a necklace, a silver belt about her waist, and on her feet tinkling anklets and toe-rings. Various-coloured glass bangles and jet bracelets decked her wrists as a set-off to the rings. Whether

---

* The *Dvipada Prabhu* has a verse which says: 'Marvellous as would be fragrance in gold.' The Telugu poets frequently mention the fancy that, were gold endowed with fragrance, it would be perfect indeed. 'Why should powder be perfumed and gold scentless?'

these jewels added any beauty to her limbs, I know not; but 'twas as plain as the palm of one's hand that the limbs gave additional charm to the jewels.

Deity, being impartial, grants perfection to no created object, but leaves each defective. So he permitted one flaw even in the beauty of Rukmini. If it may truly be called such, her sole imperfection was a rather long neck. Nevertheless, whenever Mūstiserva-sastri came for alms, he would benignly smile at sight of this same neck, and read from his book of palmistry:

> 'A long-necked wench, the sages state,
> Endows her house with riches great.'

Near by, standing in the water up to her middle and mumbling a prayer, was a widow who now and then lifted her head and poured out a libation to the sun from her joined hands with an obeisance, while occasionally she performed the triple revolution.* Some women who had just come placed their brass waterpots in the stream, and, standing upon the stones near the shore, beat out their clothes, interjecting an occasional word between the blows. An old woman having washed one half of her cloth with the other half tied about her, put on the washed portion and proceeded to drub the part that remained. Some middle-aged women, removing their jackets and other garments to wash them, wrapped about themselves on the spot the wet clothes they had already beaten out, and displayed without shame to the men who were walking on the bank or bathing in the river, those parts of the body which it is proper to keep concealed. At a distance of some twenty yards beyond, the servant-folk, occasionally lifting their hands to frighten away the crows that, cawing, flocked about the grains of refuse boiled rice, were scouring the defiled cooking utensils on the bank. Still higher up, some fishermen, clad only in scanty breech-clothes, stood waist-deep in the water, where, fastening the net-rope to the cord about their middle, they gave the net a twirl with both

---

* A religious act indicative of the omnipresence of the Deity.

hands and cast it well out into deep water, and then drew it gently in again. Others rinsed the hauled nets frequently in the stream until all the mud was gone, and pulling them to the bank, opened them with a shake that made the iron weights on their edges jingle again, threw out the gravel and rubbish, and deftly catching by the middle the little fish that here and there leapt through the meshes of the net, handed them to the lads who stood ready, basket in hand, to receive them. Half a dozen paces above that again, a lazy fellow able to earn six annas a day, mounted upon a small boat that lay in the stream and affixed to a hook at the end of a string a lump of coagulated blood, called a bait. Then standing erect he whirled the line with all his might, with his right hand cast it into deep water, and seated himself again. With undivided attention he watches the line to ascertain when a fish bites; and, whenever it shakes, starts to his feet and gently draws in the poor fish which by ill-luck has swallowed and is struggling with the hook; but, fearful that the line may break and his captive escape, he lets it run out through his right hand and then gradually winds it up as he pulls it in again; and after the fish is played out, draws it to the bank with the supreme happiness of a beggar who has found a fortune. But just as he gets it to the bank the fish snaps the line and makes off; while the unfortunate angler, abandoning the coveted prize like one who has lost his all, goes home empty-handed, grieving the more that he has lost his two-anna hook into the bargain. Near the same place some urchins on the bank tie a thread to a bamboo twig, and impaling a worm upon the hook fastened to the end of it, throw it into the stream. Pulling this out with a jerk, they seize the tiny fish and string them upon another cord, shouting joyfully to one another the while, 'Ho! I've got ten suckers!' 'Say, I've caught four sprats!' A thievish kite, perched on a tree near by looking on, suddenly swoops down upon the fish the boys have slung on the sling, and carries them off in his talons.

An elderly matron, whose whole face was one great *bottu*, removed from her shoulder a waterpot filled with cloths, and carrying it in her hand to the place where Rukmini stood, said respectfully, 'What, dear! have you condescended to bathe this morning?'

'This is *karttika* Monday,* you see. 'Tis the last Monday of the month, and so I came to bathe in the Godaveri because I must go with my mother to the Temple of Siva at dusk.'

'Can you do without your meal until evening?'

'What difference does it make for but one day? I'll manage somehow or other. Day before yesterday you said your second little girl was ill—is she any better now?'

'I don't know that she's any better. My husband has been having her exorcised by Kamavadhanulu for the past two days. We were kept awake last night without a wink of sleep until daylight.'

'Is she possessed, or what?'

'Yes, dear—what shall I say? Her husband—but there's no one near, is there?' she asked, looking about her; then coming a little nearer she whispered cautiously in the girl's ear, 'Her husband torments and devours her! You know, don't you?—it isn't two years since her wedding came off. Her husband died just six months after. Ever since then he has haunted her continually, appearing sometimes in her dreams, sometimes when she is alone at night. The child told no one, but kept the thing a secret out of modesty. For a month past he has never left her, but follows her day and night wherever she goes. What the mischief it is, I don't know: but for the last three days he has worried and tormented her more than ever. During these three days the child has been all but gone. That's the whole story! Is she never'—suppressing a sigh that burst from her bosom and wiping away a tear with the edge of her handkerchief, she paused a moment—'is she never to be

---

* The full moon of the eighth lunar Hindu month—October-November. It is a festival in honour of Siva's victory over the demon Tripurāsura.

happy with a husband? Will she never live with him?' she faltered, beginning to cry aloud.

These words touched Rukmini's heart. After a moment's agitation she made bold to say, 'You're a married woman,* you shouldn't take on so. Be quiet —be quiet, do. Does sickness leave mortals and attack trees?'

'Oh, miss, she cares for no kind of pleasure. While in such a bad way as this she's satisfied if she lives and has a cloth to put on. But as long as our two old lives last, and we have our health, she shall never want for food and clothing,' she said, ceasing to cry.

Rukmini pondered for a moment before replying. 'Somidevama, your husband's the ablest astrologer in the village, isn't he? 'Twas not through ignorance that he gave his daughter to one who lived out but half his time——'

'Yes, yes,' cried the matron, interrupting her; 'I know what you're going to say. But who is the author of his own destiny? While it is written that she's to be a widow, who can save her? People marry when they see that a horoscope is a good one; but they can't endow the bridegroom with life that he hasn't got, can they?'

'Ah, perhaps in the horoscope your son-in-law is to enjoy long life?'

After a moment's reflection the matron replied, 'Long life? Yes, it certainly is long life. Perhaps you ask, "Won't it turn out according to the horoscope?" If they fix the time properly and write the horoscope, every single syllable in it will come true. But those who don't know the science well can't fix the time properly, and so make a mess of it. Our people have determined so many periods, you see. But tell me, as far as you know, whether it has turned out differently anywhere else.'

'Your husband himself fixed the time for the wedding

---

* A Telugu proverb says: 'When the good wife weeps, wealth refuses to stay at home.'

of Kannama's Butchama in our porch; but when he wrote the horoscope of her husband, too——'

'Yes, sometimes it will happen to miss in that way. They say that the curse of Parvati* is on astrology. My husband is for ever saying so. But I hear the sound of toe-rings on the bank. Some one seems to be coming. Let's drop the subject at this,' and turning aside she set her waterpot on the bank, and waded into the stream to bathe.

In the meantime a number of housewives and widows descend the steps. Those in front, stooping down and pulling up their silver anklets a little as they approach the water, place their waterpots on the bank and turn back to talk with those near until the hindermost come up. Women, you see, never have a better opportunity to talk over their affairs at leisure than when they all come together in one place for water. For this reason it is that they usually dally a little and speak the few words they have to say whenever they come to the river.

A short female of about thirty years of age made her way to the front at that moment, and laying her finger along the bridge of her nose, called out, 'I say, Venkama! It's reported that Seshama's man beat her last night. D'ye hear?'

'Her husband's always beating her in that way. A month ago he took a stick and beat her, and broke all her bangles.'

'They say her husband don't care much for her.' Then thrusting her finger into her cheek,† she added, 'Do you know, woman, it's reported that he keeps a leman?'

A baldheaded woman came up at that moment. 'It's all very well,' said she, gesticulating; 'but is there nothing crooked in her character as well? They say her husband caught her the other day talking with

---

* The wife of Siva, and the Hindu Juno.

† The first gesture is accompanied by an expressive cast of the eye, and is used to give a hint. The second has a meaning somewhat similar to that of thrusting the tongue into the cheek.

Subbavadhani's son. It's no harm, of course, what the husband does; but the wife's conduct ought to be proper, oughtn't it?'

'What of that?' said the short one. 'But they do say that poor Chinnama's mother-in-law gives her such a time of it as never was! And besides, when her husband comes home, she makes up a lot of stuff of some kind and tells him. On the strength of this he beats her nearly to death every day.'

'Yes,' said a straw-complexioned girl of sixteen, the tears streaming from her eyes; 'wherever there's a mother-in-law alive that's the rule. If all the mothers-in-law in the world were to die at once——'

'I hear, Seshama,' said the short one, 'that your mother-in-law gives you a hard time of it too. Is it true?'

'I don't know either hard times or easy times. I'm dying because I can't stand it! I get up at daybreak in the morning, sweep the whole house clean, scour the dirty pots, draw all the water needed for the house, wash the cloths, and do up all the work by the time she rises. Late in the morning she turns out rubbing her eyes, and begins scolding me because the ladle isn't clean, or the litter in the veranda is just as bad as ever. Then until I mix the dung, stick it on the wall in cakes, and stretch my wings and come to a late breakfast, she keeps declaring the whole while she's cooking, "You're ready for your grub before there's the least sign of daylight; but you won't put a hand to the work, not you!' It's a crime, you know, if one speaks to one's husband by day; while at night after all have had dinner I must shampoo mother-in-law's feet;* and by the time she gets to sleep and I go to lie down, it's twelve o'clock. Even after I do lie down I keep starting up in my sleep to see if it is dawn, for fear that mother-in-law will get mad if the work isn't done in time. It makes no difference how I try, the

---

* A privilege of dutiful Hindu daughters-in-law.

scoldings and beatings never fail;' and she put up her cloth and began to wipe away her tears.

'Shouldn't you do your everyday work so nicely as not to make your mother-in-law angry?' asked Rukmini.

'Alas, Rukmini! you have no mother-in-law, and so know nothing at all about the matter. No difference how much work I do, mother-in-law is never pleased. When I sprinkle the cow-dung water on the floor, if I spread it thick, "Now," she goes on, "you've made a sea of the whole house; d'ye want me to slip and meet my death?" If I sprinkle it thin—"You haven't sprinkled any cow-dung water at all!—as though there was a water famine!" she jeers. If I answer when she asks me anything, she snaps me up and explodes with—"You contradict what I say?" If I keep quiet and don't answer back, she demands—"What's the reason you won't speak, you blockhead?" Do what you will when she's about, it's a mistake. If you yawn, it's a sin; if you say "Narayana!"* it's swearing. A few days ago the old cracked earthen waterpot that I've been using ever since I came to live here four years ago, went to pieces—she's abusing me yet because, she says, I broke a pot that was as new and as solid as a stone!'

'Did you never hear the proverb that says, "The mother-in-law breaks the cracked pot, the daughter-in-law the new"?' asked the short one.

'But what do you see now compared to what I had to bear? You ought to have been around when my elder brother's widowed sister was living! Since she died last year of Amma Varu's disease †—bless the goddess's heart!—I have at least rice to eat regularly three times a day. When that girl was alive I didn't have even that. I must speak what's so. No matter how bad she goes on now, mother-in-law doesn't abuse me

---

* A common *mantra*.

† Smallpox, supposed to be a visitation from Amma Varu or Kali, to whose malign influence all such diseases are attributed.

because I eat my rice regularly, but because I don't eat it.'

'If there were no such people in the world,' said the short one, 'how could the saying originate that "Even a dough image will dance for joy on its seat if called a husband's sister"?' *

An old woman who had been making her prayer while this was going on, now approached and poured out the water in her drinking-vessel muttering to herself, 'Have your eyes gone blind through the clatter of your tongues? Don't even see that there are some who have bathed over here! You don't care where you splash the water! Some of your dirty water fell on poor widowed me, who have just bathed, and here I've got to go and dip myself again till I'm like to die in the cold.' Wading into deep water she soused herself go-splash several times, and came out casting angry glances in the direction of the talkers. 'The jades are so stuck up they don't recognise their betters. A daughter-in-law hasn't a thousandth part as hard a time of it now as in my day. No mother-in-law's nice; no bitter's sweet. The wife who has no mother-in-law will be good, and the woman who has no daughter-in-law, virtuous, anywhere,' she grumbled to herself, as, dashing the river water three times on the bank with her joined hands, she proceeded a little distance, turned around thrice,† and mounting the steps passed out of sight.

'Ah,' cried Seshama, looking around in terror, 'I suppose you women'll tell some one what I've said. If my mother-in-law hears it she'll surely go and kill me. I never had much luck; but if she hears this, 'twill leave me altogether. O mother Venkama! 'twould be far better to fall into the Godaveri than to live such a life as this!' and she began to weep bitterly.

'Come,' replied Venkama, trying to comfort her, 'be

---

* The position of the elder sisters of a family is superior to that of the brothers' wives. This saying indicates the delightful tyranny of the former over the latter.

† These are devotional acts.

quiet! You shouldn't say such nasty things. The fallen are not always bad.'

'It's half an hour at least since I came to the river,' said the girl, drying her tears at this; 'she'll kill me to find out what I've been doing so long. I must go at once;' and filling her waterpot, she placed it on her shoulder and walked to the bank.

Among those who just then reached the river was a young woman of twenty summers. Pointing to the neck of another who stood near she said, 'What, Kanthama! Have you just had this necklace new-made? What do you want of it? You're a poor unlucky lass, and so your husband sets you off from head to foot with jewels!'

"'Twas only yesterday goldsmith Subbayya finished it and brought it home. He's making four strings of gold beads besides. Parama, I hear that your man's very kind to you—isn't it so?'

'What does it amount to, such kindness? He doesn't have a ten-pagoda jewel made even once a year for me to wear, not he! I suppose the sin I committed in my former existence is the reason that in this life I have such a——'

'Parama!' cried another female standing by, 'you're giving yourself needless sorrow. Do you ever want for food? Haven't you cloths enough? While your husband regards you as a queen, what's the difference if you have no jewels? What's the good of disconsolate jewels after one's husband ceases to love one? simply a useless burden! See what a lot of jewelry Bangarama of our village has. Her whole body's covered with it. I never even heard the name of some of them. But as soon as the lamps are lighted off he goes, her husband, and sits in a dancing woman's house. What happiness has she? Your husband never passes the street door after dark.'

'Oh, you're educated and can teach us all the lip-morals we need. None of the rest of us have such book knowledge as you. But when everybody else puts on her jewelry for the occasion, I'm ashamed to go to a party anywhere like a bare stick. I tell you, Jankama, if you had such a poor man for a husband as mine——'

'My good Parama, don't get angry. I meant no harm by what I said;' and filling her pot, she walked away.

The others also fill their pots with water, and pick flaws in their neighbours as they walk home.

'I say, Papama, the priest's wife, is wearing a queue over her temple.'

'Do see how gracefully the *karanam's* * girl walks!'

'I don't know what makes Ramama the Brahman's wife so proud, but she won't speak to a body at all.'

'They say that Pullama will talk with a man in broad daylight.'

'As sure as you live, Kannama's eye squints a little!'

'Sitama the *karanam's* daughter hasn't a single jewel.'

What better subjects for conversation than these have uncultivated women who know not even the odour of education? Save the quarrels of rival wives, the evil ways of stepmothers, the unkindnesses of husbands, and like matters, the women who were in the habit of congregating there had, as a rule, nothing in the wide world to talk about.

Just then a Brahman, who carried in his right hand an almanac written on *kadjan* leaves,† and wore only a waist-cloth of soft reddish tint—a small folded upper cloth ‡ was thrown over his shoulder—turned suddenly and came down the steps, after standing for a moment on the bank shading his eyes with his hand to see who

---

* The village clerk.

† Palm leaves prepared for writing upon. The almanac here mentioned is the Hindu *panchanga*, so called from its specifying *five things*, viz. the lunar day, the day of the week, the sign in which the moon is, the conjunction of the planets showing good and bad days, and the horoscopes.

‡ The usual dress of the Telugus consists of a lower cloth or girdle and an upper cloth, for which in these times of English influence a linen coat is often substituted. To these are added a turban of gold-laced cloth and laced shoes.

were bathing in the Godaveri. Both on his face and body the lines of sacred ashes were broadly visible; his rosary of *rudraksha* seeds,* each as big as a lemon, shone again; and the snuff-box tucked in at his hip swelled out like a small carbuncle.

'Rukmini,' he called out, 'make your bath. I'll repeat some *mantras.*'

'Oh, I haven't brought a single copper.' †

'Never mind the coppers. You can give them at mid-day at the house'—stooping—'make *achamana* ‡ —Kesha! Narayana! Madha! Govinda!—turn your face to the east—towards the sun.'

'Must I bathe?' asked Rukmini.

'Let me repeat the *mantra*,' said he, taking his snuff-box from his thigh and removing the stopper. Gently tapping the box twice upon the ground he sifted a little of the snuff into his left hand, and, replacing the stopper, stuck the box in the cloth at his side as usual. Taking from his left hand a pinch of the snuff as large as he could hold with his thumb and index-finger, he drew it vigorously up both nostrils, then made a second pinch of the remainder, holding it in his right hand while he wiped the left on his cloth, rubbed his nose, and proceeded as follows:

'" *On this auspicious occasion, in the reign of Maha Vishnu, on Monday the twelfth day of the dark half of the Karttika month of the year Kalayukti, I, for the improvement of my well-being, firmness of mind, longevity, health, and prosperity, bathe in the parent stream of the Godaveri, in India, the land of Bharata, on Jambu-dvipa* "—bathe three times.'

Not being in the habit of bathing frequently, Rukmini was afraid to go into deep water; so she sat down in the

---

* The seeds of the *Elæocarpus ganitrus*, used for rosaries.

† A few copper coins are usually given to such priests by those in whose hearing they repeat the *mantras.*

‡ This is a religious act. It consists of sipping water three times before religious ceremonies or meals, repeating at the same time the twenty-four principal names of Vishnu.

stream where it was not deep enough to reach to the arm—only to the knee; and, letting down her hair, poured water upon her head with her hands.* The Brahman, having repeated his *mantras*, went off saying he would call for the money. Rukmini dried her hair with the edge of her cloth and tied up her locks in its end. Glancing towards the bank she saw her father coming in the distance; and hurrying out she placed a *bottu* on her forehead with the rouge she had laid on the stone, threw water over the drinking-vessel once or twice with her hands and went back a couple of steps into the river to fill it, adjusted her cloth, and started for home with the astrologer's wife, who, her washed cloths upon her shoulder and the pot full of water on that again, had all this time been waiting for her.

CHAPTER III.

Rukmini returns Home—Description of the Dwelling—Rajasekhara returns and seats himself in his Office—Visit of Relatives—The Devotee who performs his own Menial Offices.

AFTER mounting the steps together, the astrologer's wife and Rukmini walked straight up the street as far as the temple, where they turned into a side street and proceeded for a short distance, when Rukmini, taking a couple of steps into an alley, stopped, and turning round, gently coughed twice. At this signal the astrologer's wife also stopped and looked back, and asked: 'Shall I stop, dear?'

'Do, Somidevama; I've made it necessary for you to go a long roundabout to your house.'

'How much of a roundabout? I'll walk it in a minute.'

'Please go now and come back again.'

'We're but poor folk—you must be kind to us, you know.'

* Men and widows bathe by holding the ears and nose and ducking themselves under. Married women are prohibited from bathing in this way. They must pour water over themselves.

'What does that matter? Please come,' said Rukmini, moving on a few steps, when she again looked back and called out: ' Oh, Somidevama! I forgot to tell you. When I go to the temple in the evening, won't you come too ?'

'Certainly ; that I will,' replied Somidevama.

Although neither the astrologer nor his ancestors had ever been in the habit of offering sacrifice, yet among those on Somidevama's side of the house, at least, there were not wanting some who performed their duty in this respect. It was an indubitable fact that her own paternal grandfather had sacrificed,* and by virtue of thirty-and-four sacrificial animals offered at the rate of one a year, had departed to the enjoyment of heavenly bliss with the courtesans of Elysium. The father of Somidevama did not himself sacrifice ; but being unwilling to lose in any degree the good name earned by his father at such expense, he gave to his son the name Somayazulu, and to his daughter that of Somidevama.

When Rukmini had walked up the alley for a hundred yards she turned to the south, and, after passing two doors in that alley, entered the third house by the back way.

Among the houses of the period that of Rajasekhara was considered very handsome. On each side of the street-door was an extensive *pial*.† Between these *pials* lay the walk that led within. At the end of this walk was the lion-portal, or front-door. Near the threshold there were picturesquely carved on each doorpost a lion crouching on the head of an elephant, in the act of crushing the frontal lobes. From the head-parts of these lions there was carved on each side, as far as the umbrella-board,‡ a vine decked with fruits and flowers. Upon the posts on either side were

---

* At the time of full moon in the month *Sravana* (July—August). This is among the Hindus the great day of atonement. Sacrifices performed on this day obtain pardon for all the sins of the year.

† A long, raised, veranda-like seat of earth or brickwork.

‡ A carved board placed above the doorway.

wooden horses, extending their forefeet toward the street as though about to leap down upon the passer-by. On gala-days festoons of mango-leaves are tied to the feet of these horses. Upon the umbrella-board, and directly in the centre between the two horses, was carved a lotus; and on each side of this, as far as the prancing steeds, extended a vine, clad with pretty leaves and blossoms. On this at intervals were painted parrots, their claws resting upon the vine, in the act of piercing the fruit with their beaks. Even the great nail-heads on the street-doors were chiselled over with a kind of flower.

Immediately on passing the entrance was a porch, and opposite this a great cistern. When it rained, the roof-water from all sides poured into this cistern and found its way into the street through a drain under the street porch. On the north and south sides of this cistern were two other porches facing each other. Of these the southern was the office-porch. During weddings and other entertainments the relatives and chief guests invited to partake of betel-and-leaf, sat here in a group while music and dancing went on below. When on other occasions celebrities came to call, or when, after the midday meal, some time was spent over the *puranas*,* or when pupils came to study, Rajasekhara was in the habit of sitting here. Adjoining the ends of this porch were two rooms; and on the south side was a line of double doors in the wall, which, when opened, admitted the cool mountain breeze to fan the perspiring company. Beyond these doors extended a veranda; and beyond that again a tiny area which feasted the eyes with many varieties of flowering plants. Within, on the three walls of the porch just mentioned, large pictures were hung on nails at the height of a man. Besides the Ten Incarnations, pictures of Krishna carrying off the garments of the shepherdesses and sitting in the

---

* Ancient histories or romances intended to support a creed or sect. The *puranas* generally received as authentic by the Hindus are eighteen in number.

branches of the cassia-tree while they supplicate him
with uplifted hands; dragging away the mortar to
which he had been tied by his mother for stealing butter,
thus suggesting the felling of the *maddi* trees; and
other delineations of his many pranks; Saiva pictures
representing Kumara-swami killing Tarakassura, Parvati slaying Mahisassura, and Siva destroying Tripura;
with a number of others of Ganesa, Sarasvati, Lakshmi,
and the Four-Faced Brahm, adorned the walls.* The
porch on the north side was precisely similar, except
that it had but one door, and that frequently closed.
In this porch were always one or two old palanquins
hanging up. On the floor of the porch, close to the
wall, stood a new palanquin carefully covered, and
used only when Rajasekhara went to the suburbs, or
when persons of quality asked the loan of it. Upon
passing through the door of this porch into the north
veranda, a large well appeared in the area. The wind-
lass over this well was for ever creaking under the
hands of neighbours who were constantly coming to
draw water. On the west side of the well, built apart
from the house, were two hutches for storing rice in the
husk. Near the well was a side door opening into the
street—the very door by which Rukmini had just before
entered. By the same entrance the neighbours came
and went for water; and when, during the noon hour,
the women of the vicinity came in to chat, or when it
was necessary for the females of the household to go
out while Rajasekhara was in his office, this door was
used.

The four sides of the cistern were flanked by four
pillars carved in imitation of jac-fruit. In the western
porch was a central inner door opposite that opening
into the street, and immediately on passing this another
porch appeared. This porch also had a door on its south
side. Were we to pass this door we would stand in

---

* The ten *avataras* or incarnations of Vishnu. The paintings here
mentioned depict a few of his many escapades, together with a number
of other subjects drawn from Hindu mythology.

Rajasekhara's bedchamber. There stood in this room, from east to west along the north wall, a four-poster bedstead, its feet resting in stone sockets. The bed itself was draped with musquito curtains and fringe, while between the posts were lacquered wooden salvers and caskets. A parrot's cage, ornamented with lacquered fruits and flowers, hung inside the curtains. The walls of the room were whitened with lime; and along them were arranged wall-bags—the fruit of Rukmini and her mother's diligence. A short distance above these wall-bags pretty rag parrots, tied with thread to strings, swayed in the wind. Kondapalli images and lacquered vases arranged upon a shelf resting on great pins driven into the wall, served as ornaments to the room. To the nails which supported the wall-bags were fastened small pictures of the Ten Incarnations and other subjects; and on the south side hung a Coronation of Sri Rama. When Rajahsekhara awoke from sleep his eyes would rest upon this very object—and fall on another just beyond. The room was ceiled above with a handsome ceiling. Opposite the bedstead, along the south wall, *kavadi*-boxes* were arranged in a row on the lower shelf. In these boxes were kept common, everyday clothes, and Rajasekhara's Sanskrit books written on Bengal paper in the Nagari character.† Against the western wall of this room stood a huge chest secured with a strong lock. In the small lock-boxes which this chest contained were kept the family jewels, valuables, cloths for use on feast-days, and cash. When the nights were dark, and there was much fear of thieves, Rajasekhara would spread his bed on top of this chest and sleep there. To the south, between the chest and the shelf loaded with *kavadi*-boxes, was a passage leading into the area off this room. On entering the area

---

* The *kavadi* is a sort of yoke borne on the shoulder, and is one of the most common means of transport in India.

† Before the importation of the European article the only paper obtainable in India was a coarse kind made in Bengal. The character in which the English usually print Sanskrit books is called *devanagari*, or the 'elegant.'

through this passage a broad marigold bed feasted the eyes with buds and new-blown flowers. At a little distance to the left of this again, a jasmine vine crept upon a trellis; and, although not then in bloom (that being the wrong season), charmed the sight with a wealth of green shoots.

In the porch adjoining Rajasekhara's bedroom a parrot's cage was suspended from a beam. The parrot it contained ejaculated continually in a voice of great natural sweetness: 'Who are they? Who are they?' 'The cat's come! beat her, beat her!' 'Greens here! Garden greens!' and other such expressions. A little further on were hung by cords to the same beam the Ramayana and other palm-leaf books. When Rukmini rose from sleep at early dawn, she was in the daily habit of taking the parrot from its cage, mounting it upon her hand, and teaching it all such sayings as ' In her hand a butter-pat.'

Although it was not a common practice at that time to educate women, Rajasekhara, out of love for his daughter, had himself instructed Rukmini to such an extent that she could understand a new book without assistance from others. Being of good natural ability, she derived great benefit from this instruction, and even in her girlhood acquired wisdom and a knowledge of right and wrong. Seeing him instructing her, the neighbours whispered in secret envy; but, since Rajasekhara was a man of wealth, they did not dare voice their sentiments. Neither did they remain entirely quiet. Gradually influencing a near relative of Rajasekhara's, to whom he showed much deference because of his station, they induced him on a certain occasion, when a large company was present, to broach the subject. 'Sir,' said he, 'it certainly is not customary with us to educate girls. Why, then, do you teach Rukmini to read?' Rajasekhara was a man who knew the benefits accruing from education. He was also acquainted with the fact that in no *sastra* is the instruction of women forbidden, and that the virtuous women of olden times were persons of education. He accordingly gave the question of the old man due attention, and citing a few proof passages favourable to the education of females, asked the opinion of the assembly. Those present were all men who at heart hated the very term 'Education of women;' but after they had once ascertained Rajasekhara's opinion they were not in the habit of advancing anything in opposition to it, so they flattered him that the advantages of such education were innumerable, and praised him for instructing Rukmini.

A few yards beyond the rope to which the parrot's cage was suspended, opened the doorway to the western apartment of the house. This room was large—spacious enough to seat eighty brahmans at dinner. If viewed a short time before dinner was announced, there might be seen arranged along the two walls low stools at the distance of a cubit apart, and before the stools rows of designs drawn in lines of flour. In the north-east corner of this room was an altar built of plaster. Upon this altar was a coffer, in which were kept the *salagrams*,* and other utensils used in the worship of the goddess Bhuvesvara.† On this coffer was laid a copy of the blessed Sundara Ramayana,‡ which Rajasekhara was always strict in using for the daily lesson. After coming from his bath Rajasekhara would place a stool before the altar, and seating himself, recite from the Ramayana and perform his five-fold *puja*.§ On passing out through the door opposite the altar, a paddock was entered. There, built of brick and mortar, stood a shapely *tulasi* fort,|| some four feet in height On this were cultivated with pious care a *lakshmi* and a *krishna-tulasi*. At a little distance further in the same

---

* A species of ammonite worshipped by Vaishnavas as a type of Vishnu.
† The goddess Lakshmi, the wife of Vishnu.
‡ The Ramayana is the second great epic poem of the Hindus, recording the adventures of Rama. The fifth canto of the poem is called the Sundara, or 'Beautiful.'
§ *Puja*, worship.
|| A pedestal in the form of a fort, in which is grown the *tulasi* bush.

paddock a *tulasi* plat, just beyond perennial jasmine plants, and close to these a creeping vine trained upon a broadleaved rosebay tree, afforded Rajasekhara the requisite leaves and flowers for divine worship. Here, too, arranged in rows along the wall, were marigolds and lilies lovingly tended by Rukmini and her sister. Within the kitchen area, which joined hard to the south side of the west room, plantain trees feasted the eyes with their wealth of green foliage. Here, at the very foot of these trees, Rajasekhara was in the habit of taking his daily bath.

As stated above, Rukmini, having come from her bath, poured the water which she had brought from the Godaveri in her drinking vessel upon the *tulasi* plant, then performed her devotions, and, after making the triple revolution in her wet cloth, went inside and changed that garment for a dry silk one. With a rouge casket in one hand and in the other a box containing in its various compartments some grains of unbroken rice, saffron, and rice flour, she came and sprinkled water on the altar at the base of the *tulasi* fort, cleaned it with her hands, and, sitting down, drew with the rice flour lotus designs and other curious convolutions, prettily setting them off here and there with rouge and saffron, and softly humming the while in dulcet tones the 'Fortune of the Island.'*

In the meantime Rajasekhara, conversing on various topics with those who accompanied him, and now and then asking again words lost in the noise of the many pairs of creaking shoes, came with a number of others to the house, where they, leaving their shoes in the passage, entered one after another and sat down in the office upon coloured rugs, while Rajasekhara himself sat leaning against the south wall, fanning away with his upper cloth the perspiration caused by the exhaustion consequent on walking in the sun. At this juncture Nambi Raghavacharya, pressing down the rising flakes of thick paste upon his forehead with his left hand, fixed his gaze upon

---

* A song descriptive of Rama's adventures in the Island, *i.e.* Ceylón.

Rajasekhara's face, and rubbed his hands together with a bland smile as he said:

'At present your honour doesn't show quite so much favour to Swami* as usual.' Then, rising, he drew out from his cloth a wreath of oleander flowers, and remarked as he obsequiously dropped them into Rajasekhara's hand, 'You must be very good to Swami.'

Receiving the gift with becoming reverence, Rajasekhara asked:

'Are there at present any feasts that should be observed in honour of our Janardana-swami?'

'In fifteen days,' replied Raghavacharya, 'there fall the fourteenth day of the bright fortnight of the month Margasira,† the full moon, and the holy stars of St. Mangayalvar and St. Panalvar in their order. Special feasts must then be observed. In a month's time Sagittarius will be in the ascendency. Throughout that month Swami should have daily feasts; and during the *Samkranti*‡ the feast of the Recital§ must be observed. In Sagittarius, too, the twelfth day after full moon, comes the holy star of St. Tondara-dippodiyalvar.‖ On that day we must have a bigger feast even than Swami's.'

'Does Swami have his breakfast and perpetual lamp regularly every day?'

'The two rupees your honour kindly donates are insufficient for the breakfast. At present the *swamis* are coming in greater numbers. But I keep the thing running after a fashion by adding another rupee to the one your honour gives for the lamp—for I don't want anyone else to have a share in its benefits. Swami

---

* Used here as the local deity. The term *swami* is also employed by the lower castes in addressing superiors, and especially priests.

† The ninth lunar month (December—January).

‡ *Samkranti*, the transit of the sun from one sign to another. Here used in a special sense to indicate the sun's passage from Sagittarius to Capricornus in January. This is a period of universal rejoicing.

§ A feast at which the Vedas are recited.

‖ Canonized disciples of Vishnu. Of these *alvars*, or saints, there are twelve. They are considered to have been incarnations of the attendants, arms, or insignia of Vishnu.

has no cars whatever. True, there is the *ponna* car,* but how full it will be to-morrow at the Recital! If not remedied this year, it will certainly fall to your lot next. At any rate, I thought it well to drop the matter in your ear beforehand, and so I preferred this request.'

'They say that a few days ago the priests in the temple quarrelled among themselves about something or other.'

'A priest from Dvarakati-rūmala was sitting down after dinner, when another on a visit from Pentapardu paid his respects to Bacchus and sat down too. One of them was a Tengali and the other a Vadahali; so they fell to bandying words as to whether the *pada* should be placed beneath the *nama* or not.'†

'Did it end in mere words?'

'After a while they got their hands slightly mixed up in it too; but my brother and I stepped in and put a stop to it without letting it go any further.'

'Does our Janardana-swami own no land?'

'There are said to be seven *putties*‡ of land; but a matter of five *putties* goes to the dancing women. The two *putties* that remain, too, belong to the priests and not to Swami.'

'Why, there was no music or dancing in Swami's feast that came off the other day.'

'They‖ don't come to every feast. They live in Rajahmundry, and it's very difficult to hire bandies and come down to all the trifling festivals. They come down only on the day of the car festival during the marriage of any Swami. It is the custom to give them a trifle of

---

* A representation of the *ponna* or cassia tree, carried in procession with an image of Krishna perched in the branches surrounded by the shepherdesses, whose clothes he had stolen.

† *Pada*, a mark representing the foot of Vishnu, worn by his followers on the bridge of the nose. *Nama*, a trident-shaped mark worn on the forehead.

‡ A *puttie* equals about eight acres.

‖ 'They,' the dancing-women. *Bandy*, a native cart drawn by bullocks.

four rupees from Swami's substance for their daily expense.'

At that moment a fair-complexioned benedict of some thirty years of age, dressed in white clothes and making his iron-shod stick ring again, walked familiarly from the hall into the porch, preceded by a cooly carrying a bundle of cloths upon his head, and there stopping said to the cooly:

'You, Ramiga, take the bundle inside, call someone, and leave it in Rajasekhara's bedroom, d'ye hear?'

Then thrusting everyone aside, he made his way through the company and seated himself on the carpet in front of Rajasekhara like one who had long known him intimately. Although Rajasekhara had never so much as seen his face before, yet, deeming it improper to be impolite when a person of respectability came to the house, he half rose, motioned him to be seated with a graceful wave of the hand, and himself sliding back a little way, made the stranger welcome by inquiring if all were well at home; but, fearing that his visitor might be offended should he ask who he was, he fell silent. The person who had just arrived rolled his snuffbox towards Raghavacharya, and taking possession of that worthy's box, threw away the pinch of snuff he had just shaken into his palm, took a fresh pinch with a most nonchalant air, snuffed up the half of it, and turned towards Rajasekhara with the remark:

'Rajasekhara seems to have forgotten me.'

'By no means,' replied Rajasekhara staring into his face.

'Haven't recognized me yet. You saw me ten years ago in Rajahmundry at Ramamurti's. I'm Vemarajah Bhiravamurti. We're all near relatives—the son-in-law of your worthy mother's aunt was actually the son of my maternal uncle's aunt one generation removed. Not long ago my elder brother Sambayya spent a month at your house, and after he came back kept going on continually about the kindness you had shown him. He opened his box and showed us the cloths, too, that you gave him when he came away. When I saw them

I was filled with ecstasy at the thought that you, one of our relatives, were in such a prosperous condition!'

An old fellow who was lying down in the next room, happening to overhear this conversation, coughed and came out crying:

'Haloo, Bhiravamurti! When did you come?'

'Oh, ho! grandfather Prasadaravu! is it you? Pray how many days is it since you honoured the place with your presence?' queried Bhiravamurti.

'I've been on the spot for the last two months. I came with the intention of merely paying our relative, Rajasekhara, a short visit. But I was unable to resist his importunity, and so got caught here. Rajasekhara is the best of all our relatives, I want you to know,' said he as he seated himself.

'Grandfather,' asked Raghavacharya, 'what relation is Rajasekhara to you?'

'You just heard our relationship, didn't you? The brother-in-law of his maternal uncle was step-brother to my daughter's mother-in-law.'

While this conversation was going on, a woman's voice was heard calling several times, 'Sita! Sita!' On this Raghavacharya joined in with 'Sitama!' and added, 'your mother's calling for something inside.'

A brown little miss of about seven who was playing at cowries with other girls of her age in the veranda next the well, clad in a simple skirt, and holding in her left hand the cowries that she staked at play, and in her right a bit of chalk with which she kept tally, sang out, 'Coming, coming!' and ran through the porch towards the door of the west room, making the bells upon her feet tinkle merrily. This little one was Rajasekhara's second daughter. Arrived there, Sita stopped just outside and asked:

'Mother, what did you call me for?'

'Tell father dinner's ready, and that they may go and bathe,' replied Manikyamba.

Manikyamba was Rajasekhara's wife. Although neither so intelligent nor so well educated as Rukmini;

she was yet unmatched for cleverness in the management of her household affairs and in the culinary art. In form she closely resembled her eldest daughter, except that her countenance was somewhat maturer and her complexion a shade darker. Although at least thirty-four years of age, to see from a distance she was an exact counterpart of the younger woman.

At that moment Sita came running back into the room calling out:

'Papa, mother says the dinner's ready, and that you're to go and bathe,' and proceeded to the well veranda to play at cowries as usual.

'Prasadaravu, perhaps you'll bathe. Come to the well. Bhiravamurti, are you going to the Godaveri, or will you bathe at the well?' asked Rajasekhara rising.

'As this is *karttika* Monday, I'll go to the Godaveri,' replied Bhiravamurti.

At this the whole assembly arose, took leave of Rajasekhara, and proceeded to their several homes. Rajasekhara himself walked into the west room. Manikyamba, who was inside grinding sandalwood on a stone, passed over to the door of the western area amid the jingle of toe-rings, and with one foot on this side the threshold and the other in the veranda, stood with her right hand upon the door frame and called out:

'Rukmini, your father's come to bathe; be quick and get him some water.'

Rukmini was engaged in cutting flowers for morning worship; but on hearing this summons, she called out, 'Coming!' brought the jasmine flowers and *tulasi* blossoms in a copper plate, hastily laid them upon the altar, and went into the kitchen area to hand her father the water. Manikyamba placed some unbroken grains of sandal-wooded rice in brass cups, and taking a mirror and an ash-box from their niche, brought them in and placed them beside the stool that stood near the altar. At that moment there came from within a widow of the age of forty. She had thrown

over her head a wet cloth wrung out, the pendent end
of which served as a veil. Fixing a *bottu* on her forehead with ashes from the grate, she brought some clean
water in a pair of silver drinking-cups and placed it by
the stool.

When Rajasekhara had finished his bath, he let down
and smoothed out his *juttu*,* tied the end of it in a
knot, replaced his wet cloth (which had been spread out
to dry), and entering the room sat down on the stool
before the altar. After performing the *achamana*, he
pinched off a little sacred ashes from the ball, wet it
in the water, and with the three fingers other than
the little finger and thumb, drew lines upon his forehead, shoulders, throat, stomach, and breast; then unlocking the shrine, he placed the images and *salagrams*
upon a salver and began divine worship by repeating
some *mantras*. By this time all the others had come
from bathing, and seated themselves on the low stools
arranged along the wall.

When all who were to go to dinner had gone in,†
Manikyamba left the garden, and, shutting the middle
door after her, sat down in the bedroom to fold betel
and leaf.‡ Just then, at the street door, 'Rajasekhara!
Rajasekhara!' were heard one after another a halfdozen cries like the shouts of a rustic in the fields.
Manikyamba called out from within, 'Coming! coming!'
but before she could reach the spot, there came a
fusilade of rousing thumps upon the door as an accompaniment to the shouts. When at last she got
the door unbolted, there stood by the door-post a huge
black shape wearing an old, wrinkled face, the flat
cheeks whitened by sweat mingled with sacred ashes

---

* The queue worn by all Hindu men.

† *I.e.* the men, women always eating after the male members of the family.

‡ An after-dinner refection. The nut of the betel-palm (*areca catechu*) is rolled in the fresh green leaf of the piper-betel with a modicum of slaked lime, and masticated. The preparation is highly aromatic, and very slightly narcotic. Its use stains the lips and teeth a bright red.

'There stood by the door-post a huge black shape wearing an old, wrinkled face' (p. 38).

thickly daubed upon the forehead; the earrings wagging; a head of white hair peeping out through the folds of an upper cloth in which it was wrapped; shoulders surmounted by a roll of black antelope-hide, swelled by the *darbha*-grass mat that was wrapped about the reddish tinted cloths within; and a shrivelled breast adorned with a hempen bag and a spouted pot tied to the fastening of the black hide and hanging down over the right shoulder. As soon as the door was opened, this form stalked straight into the west room, and finally stopped before Rajasekhara.

'Sastri, what is the name of your village?' cried Rajasekhara.

'Ours is Kanūragrahara,' replied the *sastri*. 'Our family name is Būlussu; my name is Perayya Somayazulu. Your fame is world-wide. Whether you give such abundant food to a dozen brahmans, or bestow alms, yours is an existence useful to the world; but what's the life of such a worthless fellow as I am good for?'

'This is *karttika* Monday. Won't you stop till night?'

'I'm an old man. I can't stop just now.'

'Somayazulu is fatigued; please go to the well and pour a few buckets of water over yourself. Dinner is just ready.'

'Let your dinner proceed. I have a request to make. I must have food cooked by my own hand. If you will have a fireplace purified with a little cowdung* and a few things got ready, I'll bathe and do my cooking.'

'There is only the one fireplace. You must oblige us by joining in our meal.'

'I'm bound not to eat women's cooking. But perhaps the persons who cook for your household are men?'

---

* Cowdung is a universal purifier among the Hindus, the cow being regarded as sacred. The floors of houses are cleaned weekly with it; mixed with water, it is used daily on front steps and before houses; its ashes are employed in applying caste-marks, and in exorcisms; while the crude article itself is one of other abominable ingredients administered to penitent apostates.

'My niece prepared the meal. In our house none but women ever do the cooking.'

'Alas, to say nothing of women's cooking, how am I to take food from a *niyogi?* * If you will have a little rice and water put on the fire, I'll come and remove it.'

'It isn't convenient to-day. You must condescend to bestow yourself elsewhere this morning,' replied Rajasekhara.

'Ah, I have it,' cried Somayazulu reflecting a moment; 'yours from the very beginning is an eminent ancestry. What a pious man was your grandfather! and your worthy father, too! He was deeply learned in theology. I have no objection to eating in your house, but if I say that I've taken meals at one place, they'll ask me to do the same at another. So if I take my dinner here, you must keep the matter a secret. This is *karttika* Monday, so I'll run down to the Godaveri and bathe and be back in a minute. In the meantime please proceed with your dinner;' and Perayya Somayazulu placed his antelope's hide and hempen bag in the middle of the floor and went off to his bath. When he returned he spread the skin in the porch, unrolled his *darbha*-grass mat upon it, and sat down. Then thrusting his hand into his bovine mask† he began telling his *rudraksha* rosary and repeating his orisons with shut eyes. Seeing him hurry like a glutton and an eater of opium, those who were seated within before the leafen plates,‡ perceiving that the rice and curry (which was already served) was growing cold, came and called him repeatedly; whereupon Somayazulu quickly laid aside his taciturnity and took his place before a platter. Then all sprinkled the *aqua lustralis* § and proceeded to take their meal.

* An inferior class of Brahmans—secular Brahmans.
† An imitation cow's face carried by such *yogis*.
‡ Brahmans seldom or never eat off metal dishes. Earthenware they regard as an abomination. Meals are eaten off plates formed of a number of leaves neatly stitched together with fine grass or bamboo splints. These are thrown away after meals.
§ Holy water sprinkled about the plates with the repetition of *mantras* to sanctify the food.

'I see nothing of Venkayya the waterman who brought the news-letter from Rajahmundry,' said Rajasekhara; 'where is he sitting?'

'Here I am, sir,' called out Venkayya; 'behind Somayazulu, at the corner plate.'

'This cooking is capital,' remarked Somayazulu; 'that of Nala and Bhima * is nowhere alongside of it.'

'Somayazulu,' remarked Venkayya slyly; 'the cucumber† you cooked in the rest-house yesterday wasn't nearly so tasty as this, was it?'

'What rest-house?' asked Somayazulu, starting.

'In Rajhamundry, yesterday,' continued Venkayya, disregarding the question, 'a merchant had a housewarming and gave a dinner to the Brahmans. Bolli Perayya did the cooking. There, too, Somayazulu and I sat in the very same row.'

Thus familiarly conversing among themselves they took their dinner, and, after washing their hands in the area off the west room, came into the porch belching and stroking their paunches, where they seated themselves. Though Somayazulu had really come with the intention of remaining several days, on the strength of what had occurred at dinner he now felt disinclined to stay, and at once partook of betel-and-leaf and went his way without even so much as asking a gratuity.

CHAPTER IV.

Reading the Puranas—The Estate of Rajasekhara—His Brother-in-law Damodarayya's History—The Story of his friend Narayanamurti—Fortune-Telling.

AFTER dining Rajasekhara had a nap, and, taking some betel-and-leaf, came and sat down in his office. Already a number of the leading villagers had come in and seated themselves in positions befitting their rank. On Rajasekhara calling out 'Subrahmanya!' a voice from

* Famous cooks of old.
† Brahmans are forbidden the use of cucumbers.

within immediately replied 'Sir!' and a fair lad of fourteen came out and stood before him. He was Rajasekhara's only son. Two years after Sita was born another boy had come; but this child was fairy-struck within ten days after his birth,* and died. After that Manikyamba bore no more children. Subrahmanya's face was unquestionably handsome, except that upon the forehead there was a somewhat ugly scar where he had been burnt with a stick of saffron for convulsions when but three years old.† His eyes were large, his forehead lofty, his locks flowing and black. On his wrists were gold bracelets; in his ears a pair of earrings set with diamonds; while a ring of fine gold-work, studded with emeralds, glittered on his ring-finger.

'Subrahmanya, what's the reason you didn't come to dinner at noon along with the others?' asked Rajasekhara.

'I thought that as this was *karttika* Monday I ought to fast until the evening meal.'

'The First Book ‡ lies just inside on the table; bring it here, and go call the *sastri*.'

Subrahmanya brought the book and handed it to his father in accordance with the command, and then passed into the walk and down the steps. Here, catching sight of a black form approaching in the distance, he called out, 'Hurry up!' and returning informed them that the *sastri* was coming, and took his seat after placing the book in the middle of the porch before the company. At that moment up came the *sastri* himself, and took a seat with the others. He had an old torn shawl folded and thrown over his shoulder, while there dangled from his ears a pair of earrings

---

* The period of ceremonial uncleanness, when both mother and child are considered to be in special danger from malign influences.

† Branding is much resorted to by the Hindus. No child escapes it. The stomach is branded for colic, the head for convulsions, head-ache, etc.

‡ The *Maha Bharata* (the great epic of the Hindus) is divided into eighteen books. The first is here meant.

that here and there, through the wearing away of the gold, showed the lac inside. Rajasekhara was himself a classical scholar; but it was counted very respectable in those days to have any celebrated book read and expounded for one by another *pandit*. Hence their waiting for the *sastri* before commencing the volume.

'Pray, why are you so late in coming to-day?' asked Rajasekhara.

'I came and looked in once before,' replied the *sastri;* 'but as they said you were not up, and I had some business to transact with another leading man, I told them I would be back again by the time you were out, and went away. A little delay took place in talking with him. You must overlook it. Master Subrahmanya, open the book.'

Opening the volume, Subrahmanya began to read the poem in praise of Ganesa * of 'the trunk, the single tusk, and the pot-belly;' and when that was completed the *sastri* himself took hold and read the 'With joined hands will I supplicate,' and other prayers to Sarasvati, various hymns in praise of Vyasa † 'refulgent-bodied as the lofty cloud of blue,' and a number of others. Subrahmanya now found the place where he had left off the previous day, and read, in that part of the book where Arjuna goes to Dvarakanagara, the stanza:

> 'My monthly vow religiously performed—
> Broad Ganga with her sacred sister streams,
> The Himalayas grand, and kindred peaks,
> But chief thy lotus feet, adored—and all
> My former sins are fled, O Achyuta!'

The *sastri* entoning this began to explain its meaning, quoting in addition some things that were and some that were not in the poem. While he was making these explanations Subrahmanya took hold of the bit of stick which was tied to the cord of the book ‡ and began twirling it about in his hand. Observing this

---

* The elephant-god, with whose praise every service is begun.
† The sage who is supposed to have written the *Maha Bharata.*
‡ The leaves of a palm-leaf book are strung upon a cord.

the *sastri* started, laid his finger along his nose, and demanded, 'Is it proper to treat the Book in that way when you're reading it?' Then he proceeded to tell those who were near a story to the effect that Vyasa actually sat upon the volume; and in reply to a question on the subject asked by some one in the company, he went on to say that unless Vyasa was actually passing by he never came into mind; and that he was then passing that very way, soaring into the heavens in his glorious chariot. And looking towards the sky, he shut his eyes and made obeisance thrice. In this way they concluded the First Book by twilight, and, bringing their reading to a close for that day, repeated the '*Svasti praja bhyaha*' * and other *slokas*, and went to their respective homes.

Relatives who were so far removed as the fortieth cousinship—some, too, for whom it was simply useless to refer to genealogical trees—bethought themselves of their relationship to Rajasekhara, and out of pure love for him kept constantly coming to his house with the modest intention of paying their respects and taking an immediate departure—only to remain for months at a time, sponging, and securing as prizes for themselves clothing and other articles. Leading men of the town and acquaintances, too, praised the capital cooking done in Rajasekhara's house, and dined there at least fifteen days of each month. Puffed up by their flatteries, Rajasekhara laid himself out to win their applause by preparing rich pastries, rice served with milk, and similar dainty dishes for them whenever they came. Even though the rice was not sufficiently boiled, or the sour sauce not hot, or the *dhal* † not browned, no one ever said that the food was not nice. Is not a dish obtained gratis always the most tasty? Some relatives when they departed would borrow a little money; and, though up to that time they had been in the habit of

---

* 'For the people, blessing!' A *sloka* is a passage of classic Sanskrit.
† A kind of pulse.

coming and going frequently, never afterwards could
find leisure to return and wipe out the debt. He was
a rich man, and everybody was his friend. But the
Goddess of Riches wholly prevented him from perceiving
whether even one of his host of followers was a true
friend or not. These excellent friends, while seeking to
rejoice Rajasekhara's heart with their praises and to
afford him the happiness of Paradise in this world, as
far as they themselves were concerned consented to
receive the money and jewels, the garments and palanquins, which he lavished upon them, simply for the
sake of his regard. Beggars without number came
daily to relate the intricate tales of their miseries, who
invariably finished up by asking him to bestow upon
them a gratuity of some sort. All the representations
of such people as these he believed to be simple truth,
and never refused them aid. Brahmans got away with
his money by representing that they were going to
make a wedding for a son, or to conduct an *upanayana;** or that they were going to offer sacrifices in
person, or to build *choultries* and feast friends.
Then there were frequently *nautches* of an evening at
Rajasekhara's house, and presentations of the 'Rape of
the Amaranth' and other plays for the amusement of
friends. Rogues, too, brought their unsaleable rings
and other articles, and by persuading Rajasekhara that
no other good fellow but he knew the value of the
stones set in them sufficiently well to buy to advantage,
sold their very words for a high rate, even though they
did not get much for the goods. Through the influence
of the priestly clique of the place, Rajasekhara had
determined to found a temple (one of the Seven *Santanas*†) and had commenced a pagoda to Anjaneya in
the vicinity of the shrine called Rama's Feet, with black

* *Upanayana*, the induction of a young Brahman into the order of
the 'twice-born,' by investiture with the sacred cord.

† *Santana, issue.* Issue has for its object the perpetuation of the
name of the person whose it is. Hence anything that perpetuates one's
name is called a *santana*. The following are held to be the principal
or *sapta santanas :* (1) Construction of a temple ; (2) The ascription of

stone brought from the Rajavara mountain. Although the work had now gone on for four years and was not yet half completed, the very workmen and sub-contractors who superintended the construction had become quite rich. He had thus got into a habit of disregarding his own wants and of sacrificing himself for the good of others; at which Prosperity became angry with him and attempted to fly away. But, unable to leave him all at once because of long acquaintance, she lingered a little longer. Poverty, learning how things stood, came occasionally and peeped in from just across the threshold—with the intention of taking possession so soon as Prosperity should give her place in the house. For the gratuities bestowed when Rukmini was married, Rajasekhara had contracted a considerable debt upon his lands. The interest of this debt was constantly growing;. but with this exception he had no embarrassments whatever.

Those who throve on Rajasekhara were many; but the principal of them all were Damodarayya and Narayanamurti. Of these two, Damodarayya was brother-in-law to Rajasekhara. Upon him they had bestowed no less a person than Rajasekhara's twin sister. She had died, however, after bearing but one son. This son was now fifteen years old. His name was Sankarayya. His mother having died before he was yet eight years old, he grew up in his uncle's house from his very childhood. It had been the desire of both his parents to give him Sita in marriage. After the death of his wife, Damodarayya had, with Rajasekhara's help, contracted a second marriage; but the girl on her wedding-day was under eight years of age, and only two years had now elapsed since she reached puberty and came to her husband's house. He had as yet no issue by this

---

a book to another ; (3) The planting of groves; (4) The construction of tanks; (5) Building a town and charitably donating houses therein and lands adjoining to Brahmans ; (6) Building *choultries ;* (7) Hiding treasure in the earth and renouncing one's claim to it for the benefit of the finder.

second wife. From the very beginning Damodarayya had been very poor; and neither was the father of Rajasekhara wealthy at the time he gave him Rajasekhara's sister. Their former place of residence was Vasantavada. There, while Rajasekhara's father was having white-ant hills dug for the walls of his house, in a certain place he came upon a treasure in a brass pot. Whether he feared he would not be so highly respected in his native place after becoming rich, or whether he feared the envy of man, is uncertain; but at all events Rajasekhara's father brought along his wife and children —his son-in-law, too—and from that time forth settled at the base of this Dhavalagiri. In this neighbourhood he acquired lands, and here, after a time, he ended his days. Until the death of his wife, Damodarayya continued to reside in Rajasekhara's house—and to obtain money from others in his brother-in-law's name and appropriate it to his own use, covering the matter up so that it might not get abroad. When, later, his creditors came and worried him, Rajasekhara himself would hand out the necessary cash. But after his twin sister died, Rajasekhara, unable longer to bear Damodarayya's irregularities, one day gave him a sound rating. Damodarayya flew into a rage at this, and proclaimed that his brother-in-law had turned him out of doors with only the clothes he had on his back. He then went off to foreign parts, allowed his hair to grow long, cultivated a beard, and came back again in six months and went about the streets in the guise of a witch-doctor with a huge rouge *bottu* on his forehead. Having before that taken good care to put the cash he had obtained in a safe place, Damodarayya now built him a house with this money and dwelt apart by himself in a certain part of that very village. His witch-doctoring proved a daily success—so much so that if anyone in the place but got a thorn in his foot, he would have Damodarayya apply sacred ashes to it. In this way he was not only becoming rich, but was also growing daily in the esteem of the people.

Narayanamurti, the second friend, had been born of a good family; but, getting into bad company, he ran through his entire fortune, and became much reduced in circumstances. Nevertheless, he still kept up an outward show of affluence. Although his fortune was gone, Narayanamurti still retained at least the outward signs of wealth; so he visited frequently the house of Rajasekhara, and requesting him to keep his secret, would call him aside, make known his need, and ask for a loan. Rajasekhara well knew that the debt would never be repaid; but he was a person exceedingly desirous of standing high in the esteem of others, and besides, Narayanamurti had been the schoolmate of his boyhood, so he would place the sum asked in his friend's hand and let him go without allowing a second party to know of the transaction. With this money Narayanamurti bought gold-laced cloths, perfumes, and other expensive articles, and made elaborate banquets for his friends. Besides this, when creditors dunned him for debts which he had contracted elsewhere, Rajasekhara at various times had paid as much as three thousand rupees out of his own private funds to deliver him from the annoyance of debt. Two years before, the wife of Narayanamurti's uncle had died without issue, and he had fallen heir to her fortune of ten thousand rupees. On hearing this, Rajasekhara was greatly pleased. He went at once to Narayanamurti's house, embraced and congratulated him on his good fortune, and declared at the same time that there was no necessity whatever for paying off the debt owing him, and that Narayanamurti must keep all his money in order to live happily and respectably. Up to that time the necessity for repaying Rajasekhara had never approached quite so near; besides, Narayanamurti now had plenty of money, so he got into the habit of telling Rajasekhara repeatedly that if he needed it, his whole fortune was at his disposal.

One day, at about ten o'clock in the morning, while Rajasekhara was seated in his office with a number of visitors, Rukmini came out to the well, and from

there proceeded to the back-door, where she stood just
inside talking with a neighbour's daughter who had
come to throw the rinds of a pumpkin she had been
peeling into the street. Just then a fortune-teller
came that way with a basket on her head and a
palm-leaf rattle in her hand. Staring into Rukmini's
face, she stopped and said, ' Miss, you're going to meet
with good luck very shortly; you're going to get a
fortune. But you've got a grief in your heart, and
you're pining to death over it. If you'll let me tell
your fortune, I'll reveal exactly what's in your mind.'
On hearing this, Rukmini called the artful one into the
yard, and made her sit down behind the storehouse
while she went in and brought some rice in a winnow-
ing basket. Taking the rice in her hand, she touched
it three times to her forehead, prostrated herself, made
a wish, and let the rice fall back into the basket. Then
the fortune-teller ran over her tutelary deities like one
who had got them by heart, begging them to be propitious, seized Rukmini's hand and exclaimed, · 'A
fortunate hand! A rich hand! You've thought a
thought; you've wished a wish; you've desired a boon;
and now you're distracted as to whether it's a green
fruit or a ripe one—a falsehood or the truth—whether
you'll get it or not. It's not green fruit—it's ripe; not
a falsehood, but the truth; and you'll get it right quick.
Perhaps you ask, "Is my thought about a man or a
woman?" For a woman it's a beard; for a man, a
lac-earring,' she ran on, watching the workings of
Rukmini's face closely. Observing it change slightly
when she said ' a man,' she at once guessed the difficulty.
' You're thinking about a man. Your wish'll soon come
to shore'; your bread's buttered,' she said, and by further
conversation learned all that was in Rukmini's mind.
Having already heard that Rukmini's husband had deserted her, 'Your man went to the bad, and is wandering in foreign parts. But he's got such a passion for
you that he'll be sure to be back after you within a
month,' she said; and taking a root from her bag, she

4—2

tied it to Rukmini's arm with a saffroned thread, received an old cloth and a jacket as a reward, and, charging Rukmini that after she joined her husband she must give her a new skirt as well, went her way. Rukmini was made very happy, and went into the house dazed, praising the skill that had enabled the fortune-teller so exactly to ascertain the workings of another's mind.

CHAPTER V.

An Attempt to marry Sita—The *Byragi's* Fame—He practises Medicine—Janardana-swami's Feast—Rukmini loses her Coin-Necklace.

ONE morning Rajasekhara was sitting in his office after the transaction of business, when the astrologer came in, and, taking a seat, drew a pair of spectacles from a plaited palm-leaf case, mounted them on his nose, passed the string back over his forehead and under his *juttu*, and loosening four or five little bits of palm-leaf that were strung on a string of a book of that material, began to swing them back and forth, gazing the while at Rajasekhara's face.

'Astrologer,' said Rajasekhara, 'what alliance is best for Sita?'

'After careful reflection it would seem that the horoscope of Mantripragada Bapiraju's son is in every particular favourable,' replied the astrologer.

Mantripragada Bapiraju had long been desirous of making Sita his son's wife by some means or other, and of profiting by the relationship with Rajasekhara. Only recently, on the celebration of the goddess Sita's marriage-day in his house, not only had he made the astrologer the possessor of a fine web of girdle cloth, but had also further excited his avarice by promising him a still handsomer present if he should arrange a match with Sita.

'Bapiraju's son is a black fellow, and besides I hear he is dull at learning. There is a report, too, that he is already walking in evil ways through the influence of bad associates. I will not give Sita to him. How is our Sankarayya's horoscope?' asked Rajasekhara.

'I have seen your nephew's horoscope,' replied the astrologer, 'and it is in every respect a capital one. But his natal star is in the third lunar mansion, while our Sita's is in the same. The *sastra* contains a *sloka* to the effect that in the harmony of these mansions destruction lurks for maid and lover: "*If the 25th, 23rd, 7th, 3rd, 5th, 14th, 13th, 12th, 20th, or 18th lunar mansions be the same for husband and wife, evil will result; but if, though in the same sign, the mansions or the quarters differ, the union will be happy.*"* The horoscope of Bapiraju's son is in every particular suitable—in it the Regent of the Trigon is in conjunction with the Regent of the *Kendra*;† but has no connection with the remaining 3rd, 6th, 12th, and 8th Regents. He is very lucky according to the *sloka* which says: "*If the Regents of the Kendra and Trigon be in conjunction, great good fortune will result, no matter what position the remaining planets occupy.*" What difference does it make about form and other trifles? Who knows how sensible a man he may become in another four years' time? Take my advice, and give the girl to him.'

'No, I'll not give the child to Bapiraju's son. When

---

* Hindu astrology divides the twelve signs of the zodiac into twenty-seven lunar asterisms or mansions, in which are supposed to reside the wives of the Moon (masculine), with each of whom their serene lord spends one day in succession on his monthly circuit.

† The annexed diagram represents the astrological *chakra* or wheel in general use among the Hindus for constructing horoscopes, and determining lucky and unlucky periods. 1 is called the *layna*, or rising sign, and with the 4th, 7th and 10th places from it, *Kendra*; while the 5th and 9th places are called *trikona*, or trigons.

my sister died, she made me place my hand in hers and promise that I would give Sita to her son. Damodarayya, too, is constantly pressing me to give Sita to Sankarayya and keep him with me. Now, in case I give the child to another, he will taunt me ever after that I did so simply because my sister was gone. Besides, our Sankarayya is a very sensible lad. He is attractive in form, and possesses both education and modesty. I shall certainly give the child to him. You must examine the horoscope carefully once more.'

Perceiving it would be of no avail to oppose this determination, the astrologer gazed for a little at the sky in meditation, and then asked, 'In what quarter* of the 3rd mansion was Sita born?'

'The 2nd quarter,' replied Rajasekhara.

'Sankarayya's is the 1st quarter. True! it is certainly auspicious. According to the *sloka* which says, "*If they who are born in the same mansion and in the same quarter thereof be married, their lives will be in peril; but should the quarters differ, the union will be auspicious even though the mansion is the same,*" not only is there no harm, but it is positively lucky. Without fail betroth Sita to him, and have them married.'

'What time in the present year would be best for the wedding?'

'Since the *sloka* says that "*The months Magha, Palguna, Visakha, and Jestha are best for celebrating matrimonial unions,*"† the month *Magha* is a favourable one. In the dark fortnight, on the fifth Tuesday, the sun is in Aquarius. That is a capital time. The *sloka* —"*When the sun is in Aries, Gemini, Aquarius, Scorpio or Capricornus, marriage alliances may be contracted; when in other signs, they are prohibited*" —is my authority.'

'Is your daughter somewhat better of her illness?'

'By your honour's favour she is much better. The

---

* Each mansion is divided into four *padas*, or quarters.

† *Magha* corresponds to February—March; *Palguna*, to March—April; *Visakha*, to May—June; and *Jeshta* to June—July.

byragi whom you recommended the other day is a very clever man. He drove the evil spirit from our house in a twinkling. All the witch-doctors had given our little one up, believing it impossible to exorcise the demon that possessed her. For three days he gave her consecrated water to drink, and tied an amulet on her arm. The child has been easy from that very time.'

'My sister Subbama is quite unwell. There don't seem to be any good physicians in our village at all, and what to do I don't know.'

'Why not get the *byragi* to prescribe for her?' asked Raghavacharya; 'he won't take money even if you offer it him. I can't tell you to how many people in the place he has given medicine out of pure charity—and cured cases of long standing, too.'

'If he is so expert, won't you bring him round to our house for a little while at noon to see Subbama?' asked Rajasekhara; 'she's been unwell for some four days past, and we're in great straits about the cooking.'

'Certainly, I'll bring him. There's no uppishness about him. No matter who calls him, he'll come.'

'They say,' observed the astrologer, 'that he possesses the art of making gold. It is simply astounding what great men there are among these Gosains!'

'It's reported that every day he melts a farthing's weight of copper and transmutes it into gold,' put in Raghavacharya; 'now and then, too, he makes donations to Brahmans. Unless he posseses the art, where does his money come from?'

'Raghavacharya, is the Swami's Recital Feast getting on all right?' interrupted Rajasekhara.

'While we are sure of your honour's patronage, what can be wanting for the feasts? Last year the *Samkranti* feast was celebrated wholly at your honour's expense. It seems only yesterday or the day before. And—to-morrow is actually the *Samkranti!* The truth is, I came to ask a favour of your honour in regard to this very matter; but as Subbama is sick, I thought it an unfavourable opportunity, and so did not mention it.'

'Last year I gave a hundred and fifty rupees; but as some weddings are about to come off among our people, I can give only a hundred this year. You must make out with that amount in some way or other.'

'Just as you think best. What does it matter about that? I'll do as you say.'

'Raghavacharya, bring the *byragi* to the house this very day without fail; and you have some other business to attend to afterwards, remember. The day is getting on—go at once. Astrologer, in case you are still in doubt, you had better examine Sankarayya's hososcope once more; and should it be necessary for you to consult with anyone, you're at liberty to show the horoscope to Lachayya-sastri as well.'

'As you please; but I have no such doubt,' replied the astrologer.

'If that is so, go home now, and come in later on.'

Thus dismissed, those present went to their homes. By the time Rajasekhara had dined and washed his hands, Raghavacharya brought along the *byragi* and introduced him to the house. Rajasekhara daily did him all kinds of good offices, and courted his favour assiduously. Notwithstanding that Subbama's illness disappeared immediately, Rajasekhara would not consent to let the *byragi* go, but, out of a desire to acquire the art of making gold, lodged him in his own house and paid him such attentions as were calculated to win his favour—supplying him with rice and milk at every opportunity, providing the fuel needed by the *byragi* to keep himself warm, and devoting himself to him in general. Several days passed in this manner, and meanwhile the Nuptial Feast of Janardana-swami approached. To celebrate this festival the people flocked in thousands from the surrounding villages until every house in the town was packed.

On the twelfth day of the bright fortnight of the month *Magha* all the requisite ceremonies of the Car

'Upon the upper part of the car where the god sat they placed the trunks of plantain trees' (p. 59).

Festival were in full progress. For four days they had been decorating the car, fastening about it cloths of various colours and bright-hued papers. To the ends of bamboo-poles they tied banners painted over with figures of Hanuman and Garuda,* and fixed these also upon the car. Upon the upper part of the car where the god sat they placed the trunks of plantain-trees bending beneath their clusters of green fruit, and tied to these garlands of mango-leaves and various kinds of flowers. Between the stems of the plantain-trees a pair of white lacquered horses faced the street, tossing their heads and lifting their feet high in the air as though drawing the car. Some ten paces in front of the car, men, thrust into distorted images constructed of plaited bamboo-splints covered with cloth and representing Anjaneya and Garuda, leapt and wagged their lacquered skulls in such a manner as to strike terror to the hearts of the children and country people who had come to see the sights. The priests hoist the images into a palanquin, descend the hill to the accompaniment of music, and seat Swami in the car after causing him to circumambulate it thrice. The crowds near pelt the god from below with plantains, while the priests and others seated upon the car ward off the blows with their hands, and ring handbells at intervals with shouts of 'Govinda! Govinda!' The people in hundreds immediately seize upon the cables attached to the huge wain and drag it along with such right goodwill that the roofs of the houses and the very street *pials* are like to fall. At that moment a musical procession stopped a short distance in front of the car, and a female put her hand to a drum and began to beat. No sooner was the roll of the drum heard, than the principal personages seated with the god came elbowing their way through the crowd, and, sending to the rear those who obstructed the way, themselves preceded the players and conducted the procession, that no interruption might occur to the music.

Rukmini, too, decked in all her jewels, and beautiful

* The kneeling griffin upon which Vishnu is represented as riding.

as a thorn-apple blossom, came that way and stopped beside a *pial* to watch the car. Her skirt fell in heavy undulating folds to her instep; over the left shoulder there came flowing down her back a gold-laced mantle woven with sprigs of lace; the dark petticoat, dotted with doves' eyes, that she wore, added a rarer grace to her beauty; the silver anklets and other ornaments upon her feet tinkled melodious music; except her right hand all the rest of her person was hidden in her mantle, but her ripe-brinjal-hued,* close-fitting silk bodice shone doubly brilliant in the soft sunshine from its partial concealment; and, to crown all, the orange-blossoms in her hair diffused a delicate perfume on the breeze, and rendered the Fragrance Bearer† worthy of his name. The women of this country, as a rule, consider it reprehensible to put on costly clothing and adorn themselves when their husbands are not at home; but when they attend a married woman's party on the occurrence of any happy event, or when they go out to witness the marriage festival of a god in the town, or the gatherings in honour of the village goddesses, they never fail to deck themselves out in rich cloths and costly jewels, even though they have to be hired for the occasion. How, then, shall I describe Rukmini's beauty at such a time? To satisfy the hunger of one's eyes they must actually behold (for no mere description will suffice) the *naïveté* of her sweet face, at that moment overflowing with the very essence of beauty. The black bands‡ encircling her large almond eyes endowed them with a rarer fascination; and the crescent *bottu* of rouge shone lustrous on a forehead that rivalled the half moon in its semblance of a smile. As soon as the car had passed her line of view there went by palmers plastered thickly over with the twelve upright marks, who, lighting lamps on iron stands and binding their

---

* Purple and gold, or warm brown.
† A title of Vayu, the air.
‡ Hindu women use a mixture of lampblack and oil to heighten the brilliancy of their eyes.

waists tightly about with their cloths, waved in one
hand whisks of peacock feathers, and with the other
dipped cloth rolls into oil, and lighting them, rubbed
them over their whole bodies with such skill as not to
burn themselves, the while receiving and throwing into
the base of their lamp-stands the coppers showered upon
them by the gaping crowd. As soon as this uproar
abated Rukmini's mother and several other women
started out together, passed the fruitstalls and copper-
smiths' shops opened in booths by people from the
neighbouring villages—threw cowries and pulse to the
shouting cripples who sat on cloths spread by the steps
at the roadsides—avoided the cunning pilgrims who,
Benares *kavadies** stuck in front and pictures in hand,
stopped those who came and went with the assertion
that they could discover saints and sinners, reveal heaven
and hell—and ascended the hill to see the god. Here
the crowd was so thick that sand sprinkled on their
heads would not fall to the ground. Stalwart men,
desirous of offering fruit to the god, forced their way
out of this living mass, and, overwhelmed in the crush
near the temple gates, concluded that while the pressure
was so great it would be as much as they could do to
escape with a whole skin, and turning back when only
half way in, fell out at the rear, no little pleased at their
release. Others more powerful than they, forced their
way to the very sanctuary itself, placed their offerings in the priests' hands, and then fell out again. The
priests themselves came out one after another, and after
wringing out their cloths (soaked with sweat) and enjoying a little breathing-spell in the cool breeze, entered
the sanctuary to swelter once more in the terrible heat.
One of the priests who had thus come out, catching
sight of Manikyamba, took the fruit from her hand and
went in and offered it to the god; then returning with
some fruit and *tulasi* blossoms from the heap within, he

---

* Ganges water is carried by these pilgrims to all parts of India, and
is highly prized by the pious.

gave these to her and placed his *sathagopa** on the head of each. Manikyamba turned back, and was about to pass the gate of the temple. Rukmini stood just behind, holding on to the end of her mother's cloth. Sita was standing on one side and an elderly duenna on the other. At that moment some one thrust his hand into Rukmini's neck from behind, and with a jerk wrenched off her coin necklace. Ere Rukmini could turn and look about her, both hand and necklace had disappeared. At her scream a dozen persons gathered around and attempted to catch the thief; but the rogue was himself in this very crowd, and joined the search for the culprit. So Rukmini and her companions returned home at nightfall greatly distressed at the loss of the jewel.

CHAPTER VI.

The Magician's Device on the Loss of the Valuable—News of the Death of Rukmini's Husband—Rukmini falls Sick—They consult a Diviner—Her Husband haunts her—Witch-doctoring—Alchemy—The *Byragi* disappears with the Money.

ONE morning, while Rajasekhara was seated upon the street *pial* cleaning his teeth, up came the astrologer in company with another Brahman and perched himself on one side of the *pial*. After eyeing from head to foot the other figure sitting profound—a silver-headed cane in his hand, his hair, beard and nails long uncut, and a great rouge *bottu* filling the space between his eyes—Rajasekhara asked the astrologer who he was.

'This worthy man,' replied the astrologer, 'is a great magician; he spent some time in the Maliyalam country, and gained a thorough knowledge of the secret *mantras*. Happening to be on the bank of the Kistna he has honoured us by coming here on a pilgrimage. His name is Harisastri. He has heretofore in various places restored lost articles in the twinkling of an eye. For the past

---

* A bell-shaped vessel graved with Vishnu's sandals. The act of placing it upon the worshipper's head denotes the remission of sins.

four years he has voluntarily lived the life of an anchorite.'*

Although the astrologer had known this worthy for only two days, he enlarged upon his history like one who could claim acquaintance with him from the very day of his birth, and recalling that verse of the *Daksha-smriti* which says, 'He who embraces the anchoritic state grows his nails and hair,' described him as above simply because he had these appendages long. Harisastri then boasted at some length of his magical power, and recited without faltering in the least, like one who had with considerable labour got them by heart, a list of localities where, he asserted, he had already restored lost articles. At this juncture the astrologer informed him that Rukmini had lost a valuable, and begged him to give them some trace of its whereabouts. Harisastri at once applied his spread fingers to the cartilage of his nose, and turned his gaze towards the sky. After counting his fingers for a moment with an air of profound reflection, he replied that the lost article had been carried off by some one who came and went about the house, and not by an outsider. Rajasekhara having by this time finished washing his face, all went inside together. Stopping in the hall, Harisastri remarked that as for restoring the lost article the whole responsibility rested upon him, and that he would come at noon and construct the magic figure, at which time all the household servants must be present. He then desired that a little rice be brought. The astrologer himself went into the house and brought the rice in a platter, at the same time calling all the menials whom he found in the house, in accordance with Harisastri's desire. Begging them to test the power of his magic, Harisastri stated that if anyone present would take an article and hide it secretly, he would tell that person's

---

* To every Brahman are ordained four *asramas*, or stages of religious advancement in this life, viz: (1) the *bramhachari*, or bachelor ; (2) the *grihachari*, or householder ; (3) the *vanaprastha*, or anchorite (4) the *yati*, or *arahat*.

name. With this remark he went out into the street. Rajasekhara handed his ring to one of the party, telling him to conceal it carefully. After he had taken his seat the *sastri* was called in and asked to point out the person who had hidden the ring. The *sastri* immediately put rice into the hands of all present, and bade them come one by one and pour it into the platter. He himself fell to repeating a *mantra*. Each one in his turn came and poured his rice into the dish. The *sastri* at once indicated a certain person to be he who had the ring. At this all present were filled with astonishment. Even Rajasekhara acknowledged him to be a great magician, and saluted him; and, believing that the lost jewel would undoubtedly be restored by his magic power, again and again begged him to come without fail at noon. He moreover charged the astrologer to be sure and fetch him. The astrologer and Harisastri wended their way homeward with smiling faces, enjoying sweet communion. Before going to Rajasekhara's house at all, the astrologer and the *sastri* had secretly talked the whole matter over, and agreed that each should have half of whatever reward he might bestow. So, after deciding privately what plan they should adopt beforehand to give Rajasekhara confidence in the magician's powers, the astrologer, before they left home at all, had settled that he was to pour his rice into the platter immediately after the person who should hide the article, and that Harisastri should then declare this person to be the party who had concealed it. Thus the *sastri* was able instantly to point out him who took the ring.

After dinner they set out, the astrologer and Harisastri, with all necessary utensils, and came to Rajasekhara's house. Already the servants and other members of the household had been summoned. The astrologer began making inquiries in a tone sufficiently loud for the *sastri* to hear, as to who had accompanied Rukmini on the occasion of the car festival, and who were by when the necklace disappeared. He then approached the *sastri* and whispered a quiet word in his ear, after which he moved off and engaged in conversation on some other subject. By this time Rajasekhara had arrived, and invited them into the house. Harisastri picked up his custodial* and withdrew, with the assurance that he would be back in a minute. After a slight delay he returned with his brass box in his hand and a copper bracelet on his right arm. A porch had been cleaned with cowdung and reserved for him. In this he drew, in lines of white, black, and green, a large figure. Placing the brass box he had brought with him on the abdomen of this figure, he opened the lid with the exclamation, 'Hail, Mother!' repeated a short incantation with shut eyes, and then turned towards Rajasekhara and desired him to bring him a sheet of white paper. At that time no paper was to be had except that from Kondapalli. Rajasekhara's son went into a room and brought him a sheet of this. While the eyes of all were fixed upon him, he tore the paper into eight equal parts, of which he laid one by his side and distributed the remaining seven among the company. By the power of the deity whom he served, he said, the name of the person who had stolen the article would appear upon that slip of paper. Placing the slip in the brass box he left it there a moment while he repeated a *mantra*, and then drew it out again and exhibited it to all with his own hand. Rubbing rouge upon its four corners from beneath, he drew upon it, with offertorial camphor, the talismanic letters and a magic diagram, laid it down, and commanded them to come and place their hands upon it in succession. Each one laid his hand upon the white paper as it lay in plain sight, and returning to his place watched with keen curiosity to see what would happen next. After all had touched the paper, Harisastri took it up, waved over it incense of benjamin, lighted some offertorial camphor, passed the slip over it four or five times, and handed it to Rajasekhara.

* A brass box for holding idols.

When he took the paper and examined it, there appeared written upon it in large characters the words 'WASHERMAN SARI.' On holding the paper up, the crooked characters were plainly visible to all; and when some one near took the paper and read the words aloud, all, with the single exception of a certain poor washerman, were filled with astonishment and delight, and fell to clapping their hands and applauding vociferously the *sastri's* skill and power of divination. Some who were present began to accuse the *sastri* himself of being the thief, and to assert that he was standing just behind when the necklace disappeared. But Sita declared that on that occasion Sarvi-gardu stood in their rear with some fruit in his hand; whereupon all concluded that the person who had stolen the jewel was none other than Sarvi-gardu the washerman. Rajasekhara and all the other members of the household believed the same. But when they demanded that he hand over the lost article instanter, the washerman, with tears flowing in one steady stream from his eyes to the floor, began to swear by his wife and children that he knew nothing whatever about the theft. Everyone knew, of course, that these were only crocodile tears; yet, notwithstanding all their threatening and coaxing, he still, with tears, declared that he was innocent, until finally Harisastri drew Rajasekhara aside and intimated that he had but to say the word and he would mesmerize the washerman and so make him restore the missing article. As the washerman had done his work most faithfully from his very childhood, Rajasekhara was unwilling that any injury should be done him, and simply dismissed him from his service. The washerman went to his home weeping, and declaring himself innocent. What the astrologer had in the first instance whispered in the *sastri's* ear was an intimation that he should write the name of the washerman Sarvi. When, however, he withdrew on a pretence of fetching his custodial, he had written on a slip of paper with onion-juice the words 'Washerman Sari,' omitting the *v* through ignorance of spelling. After drying this slip and placing it in the box, he returned. When Raja-sekhara's son brought out the paper, the *sastri* tore it into slips. When, however, he put this into the box, he changed it, and drew out the original paper. As the two papers were exactly alike, no one had the least suspicion. His writing the magic letters on the paper with the offertorial camphor was for no other purpose in the world than to get rid of the smell of the onions. Smoking it afterwards in the benjamin fumes and over the camphor, was a device for bringing out plainly the letters which did not already show. In recognition of the brave deed which Harisastri had thus performed by the power of his magic, Raja-sekhara tied about him a web of girdle-cloth, and presented him with four rupees in cash, and that, too, notwithstanding the fact that the lost necklace still remained unfound. On returning home the *sastri* and the astrologer divided this reward of their services in equal shares.

When the sun was about three hours high on the morning of the day following these events, Rukmini was sitting alone in the veranda of the west room worrying over the loss of her jewelry, and reflecting with mixed feelings on the fact that though the period fixed by the fortune-teller had expired the very day before, her husband had not yet returned. At that moment a young man of about the age of twenty walked in, and, throwing down the bundle of clothes which he carried in his hand, gazed into Rukmini's face and burst into a flood of tears. Seeing this Rukmini herself fell to weeping, although wholly ignorant of any reason for so doing. The inmates of the house, hearing the sound of wailing, came running out to inquire what the matter was. The young man choked his tears, and in reply stated that Nrusimhu-swami, Rukmini's husband, while coming from Kasi had, on the way, at Jagannadham, on the ninth of the bright fortnight of the month *Pushya*, paid the debt of nature, and that he himself had performed the crematory and other ceremonies. No sooner did they hear these words than the whole household with one accord fell to weeping uproariously. Rajasekhara, who was in his office, and the inmates of the neighbouring houses, hearing the sound of lamentation, came in and joined unreservedly in the family grief on learning the calamity that had befallen them. Those present who were more advanced in years then had them all bathe, consoling them the while by quoting scripture texts. After several days had thus passed a number of relatives and friends spoke to Rajasekhara about removing Rukmini's hair; but out of love for his daughter he would not consent to have that act performed while she was so young; and all were fain to concede that no trouble would arise from the omission, and that the course he had chosen was best.

The mind even of an enemy cannot but be shocked at the bare thought of the wretched condition, in this country, of women who have lost their husbands. The very parents who should console and aid them in forgetting grief for their husbands, pitilessly make the daughters whom they bore—now overwhelmed in a sea of sorrow at the loss of the lords of their life—aliens to all adornments, disfigure them by shaving their heads, and force them to sit, veiled, in a corner. They shrivel them up by neglecting to provide regularly even sufficient food to satisfy hunger, throwing them only a few grains of boiled rice in the afternoon when all the rest have dined. They permit them to wear no decent raiment, even though they desire to do so, allowing them only a coarse cloth without a border. Why a thousand words? The lives of those bereft of their husbands they make very vessels of sorrow, and lay them by like living corpses. Modest women regard death itself as preferable to surrendering to the knife of a heartless barber the beautiful tresses which, given by no earthly hand, were bestowed as an ornament at their very birth by the Supreme One, and which, from earliest childhood, they have oiled and combed and cherished as they have life itself. All the hard and mean work of the house falls upon them. No sooner do they reach the home of their birth, than elder brothers' wives and younger brothers' wives regard them as slaves.* On festal occasions, so far from tolerating their mingling on terms of equality with others—let them only so much as show their faces and everyone abuses them for birds of ill omen. For these reasons the very term 'widow' strikes like a keen dart upon the hearer's ear. But call a female a 'widow,' and she at once flies into a towering passion at what she regards as a frightful piece of abuse.

This whole state now appeared, as it were, before her very eyes; and from the day she received the above intelligence Rukmini took to her room and left it neither day nor night, abandoned both food and sleep, and began to grieve and pine for her husband. Along with her sorrow some sickness or other also fastened upon her; but until she became so weak that she was unable to rise, no one discovered this fact. As soon as it became known, however, Rajasekhara called one Basavayya, a Jangam who was celebrated as an excellent physician, and showed him the sick girl's hand. Seating himself upon the cot where Rukmini lay, he took her left hand in his, and remarked that her pulse indicated fever. She had had, he said, the ague for several days, and, as they had not discovered it at once, it had become deeply seated. Quoting from his book of pharmacy the *sloka*, '*Mercury, cassia chips, rue, dry ginger, long pepper, black pepper, mace . . . root of nightshade, cobwebs, ground and black tulasi, betelnut, green paun-leaf . . . leaf of the chaste tree . . . and stems of ripe banyan-leaf, break up ague,*' he wrote these ingredients on paper, and for the time went home. By

---

* On the death of the husband, the wife, if young and without children or property, returns to her father's house. Here, owing to the prevalence of community of goods among the Hindus, there may be several brothers' families.

mid-day Rajasekhara had obtained all the necessary articles and sent word to the doctor; who, when he returned, had them triturated, made them up into powders, and told them to administer three powders three times a day with honey as a vehicle. As for diet, he prohibited only oil, pumpkin, spinach, acids, roots, and jac-fruit. He continued his visits in this way twice a day, examining her pulse and observing her symptoms. At first Rukmini's condition slightly improved; then delirium and other bad symptoms set in at night, and the fever began to grow steadily worse. When they called the doctor in and demanded why it had not yet abated, he quoted the words, 'A fever contracted when the moon is in the 27th or 17th lunar mansion continues for many days,' and stated that as this fever had set in under the 27th mansion, it would not soon be got rid of. Rajasekhara's confidence in this man's word was now pretty well shaken, and he called another doctor who practised in the place to see Rukmini. He felt her pulse and at once pronounced it to be bilious fever; but he asserted that in thirty-six hours he could make Rukmini's a constitution strong as adamant. Possessing, however, a larger stock of words than of drugs, he took refuge in a certain rule which says that 'Abstinence from food is the supreme cure-all,' and began to appoint her fasts. He declared incessantly that the fever must have its course for nine days; but seeing Rukmini waste away and grow weaker and weaker day by day, they paid no further attention to him, but abandoned his treatment and called in the first doctor again. He immediately regulated the diet and began the use of medicines as before. Through the efficacy of his prescriptions the disease at first gave some slight indications of turning; but it eventually proved to be not one whit the less virulent.

Meanwhile Manikyamba, actuated by love for her daughter, rose one Sunday morning at four o'clock, just as it was breaking day, and taking Subbama with her, and starting so that they should get there before anyone else, went herself to the Temple of Koralama* to consult the oracle. When Manikyamba had burned incense, the *pariah* woman in charge of the temple placed herself *en rapport* with her patron deity, and impersonating Rukmini's husband, wailed out that he had died like a mateless bird in an evil land, and affirmed that out of love to Rukmini he had now come to take her to himself. At this declaration both Manikyamba and Subbama fell to weeping. After their grief had somewhat abated they gave the *pariah* woman the customary guerdon and went home.

Both at night in her dreams and by day when she shut her eyes, Rukmini's husband now began to appear to her. Sometimes, too, she heard him as it were talking to her; but she could not comprehend his words. Now and then she would cry out in her sleep, thinking that some one was seated upon her breast.

While matters were in this state Harisastri one day returned in another guise, and after examining Rukmini's pulse averred that it indicated demoniacal possession. They had the *byragi* apply sacred ashes and administer draughts of holy water; but Rukmini did not appear to derive the slightest benefit from this treatment. One day there came along a mendicant playing the *dakka*.† In his head-cloth was stuck a bunch of bird's feathers, a bundle of canes was swung over his shoulder, and on his back, suspended from the canes, hung a huge leather bag. On Manikyamba asking an augury, he looked into a palm-leaf book decorated with lines and figures, and said that on the day they went to the feast a wraith had alighted from a *juvvi* tree and taken possession of her daughter, but that it would leave her if exorcised with the lamp. He gave her a bit of root, and instructed her to put it in

---

* A village goddess. Their number is legion, and their worship very common among the lower castes.

† A small double drum-like rattle. A tiny ball of earth is fastened by a string to the centre, and made to strike each side in succession by rapidly twirling in the hand. These mendicants are called *buda budakkas*, perhaps from the noise made by this instrument.

a silver amulet and tie it to the fleshy part of the girl's arm. Thereafter he went his way with a rupee as his reward.

Manikyamba accordingly exorcised Rukmini with the lamp, but no good resulted even from that. One day Subbama, going into a trance, impersonated Venkatesvara, and declared that the whole thing was the result of his power; but if the mother, he said, would come to the hill and worship, vowing to him her ornaments and habiliments as she stood, all would turn out well. Manikyamba accordingly prostrated herself before the mountain god and vowed one of her jewels; but notwithstanding all this, Rukmini's health improved not a whit.

Harisastri then declared upon his honour that he would cause the demon to speak through the girl, and drive it out that very night. Ere the sun was yet two hours high he was on hand, and, after having the porch cleaned with cow-dung, drew the figure of a woman the full length of the floor in coloured lines, and so distorted that the bravest might well tremble at sight of it. After taking a bath he shook out his *jutta*, and plastered his face all over in one great saffron *bottu*. He then had Rukmini bathed and placed in the midst of the drawing in her wet clothes, and rubbed sacred ashes upon her face and stationed men all around to make kettle music. Touching her forehead with lamps so bright as to dazzle the eyes, and burning incense of such potency as to intoxicate even those who were well, he pronounced the cabalistic letters in a voice so loud as to make the children in the neighbouring houses quake, and seizing a cane fell upon Rukmini with eyes glaring as though about to beat her, shouting, 'Tell the truth as it is!' Rukmini had already lost consciousness, and was wildly gazing about her; so she affirmed, in accordance with what her mother had said after consulting the diviner, that she was Nrusimhuswami; that his love for his wife being insatiable he had taken possession of her; and that he would shortly take her away with him. The *sastri* then rubbed something on her face to counteract the intoxication, and bade those who stood about carry her in as soon as she had regained consciousness, and apply cooling lotions. These directions given, Harisastri went home for the time. All that day and the next Rukmini lay weak and insensible. The next morning Harisastri again put in an appearance. The spirit that had taken possession of Rukmini was, he said, a stubborn one. It could be exorcised only by means of the supreme *mantra*; but he would yet drive it out even though he had to call into requisition the merit of all the austerities he had ever subjected himself to. He accordingly directed Rajasekhara to get ready ere night nine cubits of new cloth, a *maund** of *ghi* for the lamp, some flowers, six cubits of hempen rope, a few nails, and a brass vessel capable of holding a couple of quarts of water, and to have a room with but one door cleaned with cow-dung and held in readiness. Rajasekhara prepared everything carefully in accordance with these directions, and sat anticipating the *sastri's* arrival. It was after nine o'clock in the evening when Harisastri returned. He at once lighted a lamp in the room and placed his custodial near it, and, after drawing in the centre of the room a small design with rice-flour, seated Rukmini on it and mumbled a *mantra* for a moment. He then by a magic rite closed the four quarters of the heavens that the demon might not escape, sprinkled charmed water in the corners of the room, and commanded those present to take Rukmini out. When they had removed her he bolted the room door on the inside, but after a little came out and locked the door behind him. The spirit, he said, had during its lifetime gotten possession of the *Nrusimha-mantra* and would not give in to any deity whatever. By exerting his whole strength he had merely succeeded in binding it so that it should not leave the room. If, however, he used the griffin *mantra*

---

* Twenty-five pounds.

from the outside, it might succumb after a hard fight, but in no other way was the thing possible. He at once began the repetition of the griffin *mantra*—'*May you, most horribly mangled, become food for the griffin, the king of birds, the destroyer of all enemies, existent in the cabalistic characters Om, Khim, Kham, Ghrasi, Hum, Phat.*'

By the time he had twice repeated the incantation there were heard from within the room blows as of one person beating another. Then followed a heavy thud. The blows continued distinctly audible for the space of half an hour, when the noise ceased, and Harisastri, affirming that the spirit had been very easily caught, and that he must at once take it and blend it in the Godaveri, went alone into the room, gathered up all the articles it contained, and carried them off. From the following day Rukmini's sickness gradually abated and she began to grow rapidly better. Later, the Brahman directed them to take a copper plate, draw on one side

10	5	16	3
15	4	9	6
1	14	7	12
8	11	2	13

of it a figure of Anjaneya and the essential letters, and on the other a diagram (as here shown) containing fourteen squares numbered in such a way that they should amount to thirty-four however added. If this amulet were tied to Rukmini's neck, no manner of spirit could do her any harm so long as it remained. Rajasekhara, in addition to giving the *sastri* a length of girdle-cloth for freeing his daughter from the demoniacal plague, made him a donation in addition of one hundred and sixteen rupees.

When the *sastri* brought his image box that night he had in it only a few stone idols. When, after sending everyone out, he sat quite alone in the room, he shut the door, drove the nails into the middle of the mud ceiling and tied the hempen rope to them, tore off a small piece of the new cloth and knotted the stone images in this at short intervals, dipped the cloth freely in the *ghi* and tied it by one end to the hempen rope, filled the vessel with water on the ground directly beneath it, spread the flowers neatly over the surface of the water, touched the lamp to the end of the cloth, and came out to await events. In two or three minutes the drops of burning grease with which the cloth was soaked began to drop into the water go-tap, producing a sound as of blows falling upon a human body. When it had burnt up to the stone images, these loosened and fell into the water with a loud noise; but owing to the flowers with which the bottom of the vessel was covered, it did not sound at all like the clang of brass. After the cloth was quite consumed the *sastri* went in and gathered up the soot and rubbish clean, and carried away all vestiges of the deceit he had practised.

Actuated by a deeply-seated desire to acquire the alchemical art, Rajasekhara still continued his constant attentions to the *byragi*, and courted his favour with an eye open to the coming opportunity. One day while the *byragi* was taking his ease after his morning repast, Rajasekhara approached and addressed him deferentially.

'Bavaji, is there such a thing in the world as the art of making gold?'

'There is,' replied the *byragi*, with a low chuckle. After some further conversation Rajasekhara clasped his hands with supreme reverence and devotion, and asked: 'Of what nature is this art?'

Thereupon replied the *byragi* that 'that was the supreme arcanum; yet would he reveal it to him;' and went on to relate that in bygone ages iron was turned into gold by means of the philosopher's stone, unknown in this, the Iron Age; that of old Sankaracharya * taught the art

---

* A disciple of Vishnu, and the originator of the *shanmatas*, or six creeds, in vogue among Hindus. He stands at the head of the Vedic

of transmuting metals to a toddy-drawer who made gold at pleasure, and at last joining the Yogis, communicated the secret to them and gave up the ghost; that his own preceptor had instructed him in this same art, but as the disclosure of the necessary *mantra* had been incomplete, it had never proved of any use to him; and that he could now make gold by means of vegetable saps only. All this as though he uttered it simply as a favour to Rajasekhara. As everyone, he said, would pester him to make gold, he desired that the matter be kept a profound secret. Rajasekhara bound himself to preserve the secret as desired, and prayed the *byragi* in many sorts to confide to him without delay the recipe for making gold. But to this the *byragi* objected. Householders, said he, must not employ this art; if they did, they would suffer loss of family. He would himself, however, make gold, and give it to such as had confidence in him; but he could on no consideration disclose the recipe.

Rajasekhara now conceived the notion of at least having some gold made for himself, and patronized the *byragi* with greater assiduity and reverence than ever. While he was one morning sitting with the *byragi*, after presenting him with some milk and sugar that he had brought, that worthy—the workings of whose face indicated that Rajasekhara stood high in his favour for the nonce—asked him to fetch two annas' weight of gold and a like quantity of silver. When he had brought these, the *byragi* tied both together in a rag, which he then proceeded to place on the coals before Rajasekhara's astonished eyes. After allowing it to remain in the fire for a moment the *byragi* squeezed out upon it the juice of a leaf, and after waiting a little while removed it with a pair of tongs, and placed in Rajasekhara's hand four annas' weight of gold. This only served to render him the more eager, and he begged the

---

system, and is the author of a celebrated commentary on the Sutras of Vyasa. He is said to have been born about A.D. 100.

'When he returned fan in hand, the byragi was blowing the fire through a bamboo joint' (p. 79).

byragi again and again to combine all the gold and silver he had in the house and turn it into gold at a stroke. He repeated this request with so much persistency that at last the Gosain gave ear to his prayer, and set him to gather together all the gold and silver in the house, and fetch it to him in a bundle. In accordance with this command Rajasekhara collected the jewels of the household, the silver plate and the cash, tied them up in a huge bundle, and brought them away to the *byragi* so secretly that not a soul in the house knew anything about the matter. The *byragi* immediately made a fire of cow-dung cakes, and had Rajasekhara place the bundle upon it with his own hands. He then covered it up and sent Rajasekhara into the house to bring a fan. When he returned fan in hand, the *byragi* was blowing the fire through a bamboo joint, and the bundle was plainly visible through the interstices of the dung-cakes. After throwing on a few more cakes and making a blaze, the *byragi* rose with the remark that he must go and fetch some necessary roots from Vamagiri, for unless he brought them in person and expressed the juice, the whole would not become gold. Until he returned Rajasekhara was to pile on the fuel, keep up the fire, and watch the bundle carefully. With this injunction away went the *byragi* for the roots, and though he failed to put in appearance again, Rajasekhara stuck to the spot and sent men to call him. They searched the whole hill, and, finding no trace of him there, supposed he had gone to some more distant hill for some scarce herb that he was unable to find, and accordingly returned to the village with this piece of information. The *byragi* did not return — perhaps because he failed to find the roots which make gold. Rajasekhara waited for him a whole day, when, on opening out the fire, he found in it, not gold and silver, but a simple white calx. Delighted that the silver had so easily been transformed into calx of gold, Rajasekhara concealed it carefully; but, for some reason or other, this substance seemed to possess neither weight nor any other characteristic of the calx of gold and similar metals.

CHAPTER VII.

Rajasekhara's Poverty—Death of Subbama—Conduct of Friends and Relatives—Journey to Rajahmundry—Bathing during the Eclipse.

WHEN Rajasekhara read, '*Griefs and ills by the hundred destroy human happiness; but where wealth is, there enters as through a wide-open door the most baleful calamity*,' and other *slokas* which teach that money is the root of all evil, he often used to yield to the influence which pious books exert, and long for poverty. Unlike Lakshmi,* her worthy sister is ever easy of access; so, no sooner did he frame the wish than the Goddess of Poverty immediately appeared and gratified his desire. Yet did not poverty seem quite so sweet after all as he had long anticipated. He had not now the wealth to bestow in charity that he formerly possessed, and consequently the host of blatant flatterers who had hitherto been in the habit of lauding him for an Indra and a Chandra,† gradually deserted him and began to curry favour with those who had become rich and prosperous by his aid. Yet was Rajasekhara unable to send away empty those who begged of him with outstretched palm, but denied with his hand itself what he could not refuse in words, setting before those who asked a meal such food as he had. (For this reason it is that the happiness of the hospitable man, be he never so poor, is always gauged by his poverty.) But none of those seeming friends who had formerly condescended to grace his feasts with their presence, now took any pleasure in them. Even for these charities some means was essential; and for a time Rajasekhara obtained money by pawning the brass utensils belonging to the house. Thus the household furniture diminished day by day, and the responsibility of guarding it grew light. After things had moved on in this way for a time, nearly

---

* The Goddess of Wealth.
† Indra, the Hindu Jupiter; Chandra, the regent of the moon—Adonis.

all the movable furniture about the house became transformed into baskets and hampers and wooden-ware. Being even then unwilling to cause pain by refusing anyone who begged of him, he began at the instigation of the Goddess of Poverty, and in spite of the fact that he had never before so much as known the word falsehood, to give empty promises instead of gifts. Surely there is no more potent agency than poverty in causing men to commit evil! For, though suffering thus keenly, he practised a certain amount of dissimulation, and endeavoured to hide his poverty from the eyes of others by wearing good clothes even at the expense of a less generous diet, and by giving to the poor, even though he went in debt for the means. What delusion it is, I know not; but mortals the world over take much more pains to make others think them happy than they take to actually attain to that desirable condition. Although the Scriptures paint in glowing colours the pleasures and advantages accruing from poverty, and abuse wealth as the root of evil, poor Rajasekhara thought each moment an age while asking himself whether this Goddess of Poverty would never take her departure. He now began in consequence to supplicate more and more that Goddess of Fortune whom he had before regarded with indifference. But the more enamoured he became and the more assiduously he wooed, the farther did the coy goddess recede.

Just then, of all times, Subbama fell sick again. Rajasekhara now got out of all patience, and rated her soundly for falling sick and causing him greater expense by her fasts and fooleries, her twenty baths daily, and her sitting around in wet cloths, at a time when he was so hard up for money. A Brahman who had come seeking work, and was going away disappointed, happening to be near, overheard this rencontre, and telling Rajasekhara that it was useless to abuse her, declared he would himself set to as a Brahman cook, and that they might let her stay sick as long as she pleased; and, in fine, showed plainly that so long as he was there, who could surpass either Nala or Bhima in the culinary art, she might even die, if she wished, for all he cared. How much of truth his words contained will never be known ; but at all events—whether because there was no skilled physician available, or because it was the duty of this same Brahman to superintend her food and drink—the disease grew worse, and Subbama was one day found to be *in extremis*. The family priest declaring the astral influence to be bad on that particular day, they carried her into the street and made her a bed on the ground by the side of the wall, tying up a mat to shield her from the gaze of the passers-by. That night, about nine o'clock, she—*mirabile dictu*—passed into the other world. All the members of the household held wake over the corpse that night until break of day, when, though they made every effort in their power from early morning, not one of the Brahmans in the village would come to their assistance. Rajasekhara then started out himself, and happening to find a bearer of corpses in the house of a dancing-woman, acquainted him with the circumstances; whereupon he fell to bargaining for the job, and, after finally consenting to carry the corpse to the burning ground for the small sum of sixteen rupees, rose and followed Rajasekhara.

It is a fact disgraceful to the whole Brahman caste that, even at the present time in the Telugu country, when anyone dies in the house of a Brahman, and more especially in the house of a *Smarta*,* his relatives and fellow-sectaries not only will not come and lend their assistance, as in other religions, but even though one go and implore them, actually make many excuses for their non-attendance, and conceal their faces from view. Where none will assist in this the most dreadful of all calamities, what is the advantage of embracing a religion ? Or what harm can result from not professing any ?

By the time the corpse left the house that day, it had

---

* The highest sect of Brahmans.

gone twelve o'clock; and when they reached home after performing the cremation, the sun was but two hours high in the west. Then followed the *sanchayana*,* and all the other obsequies prescribed by the rubric.

Friends and relatives now ceased to visit Rajasekhara as frequently as before. When they met him in the street, too, they attempted to pass by as though they did not see him; and when there was no alternative but to stop and talk, they cut the conversation short with two or three words. Those who formerly praised him to his face when he discoursed, now either manifested their assent by a mere shake of the head, or began to listen to his utterances with sneers. After a while both the headshaking and the sneers ceased—or rather passed into inattentive humming and hawing; and in course of time even these died away and gave place to all kinds of satirical remarks. Though both Rajasekhara and his wife and children were penniless, they inwardly derived no little comfort from the reflection that at least they had not squandered their wealth for any evil purpose, and were in consequence content with what little they had left. There were some, however, who perceived, and were unable to endure their happiness. These envious ones came to them under the cloak of friendship, and destroyed their peace by asserting that this, that, and the other one was slandering them. The very individuals who a thousand times before had praised Rajasekhara's liberality as largess, now began to condemn it for a sinful waste. Even they who had formerly reaped innumerable advantages off him, began now to point the finger of scorn when he passed along the street, and to jocosely inform the bystanders that this was a man who had squandered his whole fortune and become a magnanimous vagrant. Damodarayya, even, who used constantly to press him to betroth Sita to his son, now affirmed in the presence of various parties that he would never marry his son to that girl. When

---

* Collecting the ashes and bones of a burnt corpse.

this report reached Rajasekhara through a series of ears, he one day went and asked Damodarayya if it were true; he replied curtly that he would not have the ceremony performed that year. The very astrologer who, in writing Subrahmanya's horoscope, had asserted that in the whole world there was no one so lucky as he, went to the parties who had promised their daughter to the lad and made them refuse to give the child, by affirming that Subrahmanya's, of all the horoscopes he had ever seen, was the worst. Though suffering thus keenly from want of money, Rajasekhara was unwilling to borrow of others, and endured the misery of his changed condition stoically. Thinking, however, that he surely could not be without at least one true friend, Manikyamba and Subrahmanya approached him with the supplication that he should ask a loan either of Narayanamurti or some other person, and so obtain a little money for Subbama's *masika*.* Unable to deny their request, he sought an opportunity and asked Damodarayya, Narayanamurti, and a few others who had profited by him while conducting themselves as friends, for a loan. But these persons who formerly, when he did not want it, had been in the habit of declaring again and again, unsolicited and with every manifestation of pleasure, that they would be only too happy to let him have a loan, trust them for that!— now that he really needed it, made a thousand excuses, and regretted they were so short of funds. Though the majority ceased coming to Rajasekhara's house, a few, for a brief period, still continued to visit him. But these also, through fear that he might ask a loan of them, soon dwindled away, and Rajasekhara's dwelling, that had previously been constantly thronged with guests and filled with uproar, was left destitute of people to strut and stare, and became silent as the grave. But it did not long remain in this condition. What magic

---

* A monthly ceremony for a deceased relative, continued for a year after the death.

there was in the planting of its roof-tree,* I know not; but after a little it again became filled from morn till eve with men, crowded more closely than ever, and once more re-echoed to the sound of many human voices. Formerly it had overflowed with persons who, thinking one thing and saying another, acted with duplicity, and with poor people begging food and clothing. Now it was packed with straightforward individuals who had no hesitation in speaking out fearlessly what was in their minds, and with persons of wealth who demanded authoritatively the money due them, with which to buy food and clothing. Rajasekhara's goods, too, began to multiply day by day in such a manner as to keep the house crowded; for, although there was not so goodly an array of eatables as formerly at the morning meal, yet these were still Rajasekhara's chief care; and in his nightly dreams, at least, were a thousand times more abundant than ever before. While he was hedged in by these troubles, the same learned Brahmans who, only a short time before, had commended him for not suffering Rukmini's hair to be removed, now abused him right and left, and attempted moreover to frighten him with threats of writing to their priest, Sri Sankaracharyaswami, and having him expelled from caste unless he paid their clique a gratification of one hundred rupees. Because his home, thronged with creditors, was like a wilderness; because the village, filled with magnanimous souls who mocked at him and declared even his good qualities to be bad ones if he went into the street, was like a great sea; and because even death itself seemed preferable to a continued but ignoble existence in a place where he had so long resided respectably—he determined by hook or crook to pay off all his debts, leave the village, and take his departure to another place. Without delay he went to Ramasastri and raised five hundred rupees by mortgaging his house, entering into a bond to return the money in a year's

* A preliminary ceremony in building a Telugu house is the setting up of a pole at a time favourable for the commencement of such work.

time with interest; or, in the event of his being unable to repay the money within the period named, to make over the house to Ramasastri. With four hundred rupees of the money thus obtained, he wiped out all his debts. From the very day following that on which he gave the loan Ramasastri kept sending messages to the effect that he must at once clear the house and give him possession. Ever since first reading the *Skanda Purana*,* Rajasekhara had cherished a desire to go on a pilgrimage to Benares. Rejoicing that his desire was now, in this way, to be gratified, he determined to set out with his family for the purpose of bathing in the Ganges; and, after fixing a time for the journey under a certain peregrinatory sign,† when the influence of both moon and stars was favourable, he observed the caution, 'On the 1st and 9th, on Saturday and Monday, journey not to the east,' and obtained a cart with the intention of starting at two o'clock on the afternoon of Wednesday, the 13th of the light fortnight of the month *Palgu*. Their only pilgrimages up to that time had been from the bank of the Godaveri to the house, and from the house to the bank of the Godaveri; but farther from home than this they had never travelled before.

When Rajasekhara had brought the cart and tied it at the door, he charged them again and again to get all necessaries into it before the time fixed for the start went by. Manikyamba at once began bustling about, and packed the bandy full of lime baskets, hampers, and palm-leaf buckets, at the same time heaping in the street-door enough to fill a second cart. All the brass vessels and clothes-boxes which were to go in the bandy

---

* The second of the eighteen principal *puranas*.

† Hindu astrology divides the zodiac (which corresponds exactly to that known by us) into three equal parts of four signs each (*kandayas*) with reference to their supposed influences, as Aries, Cancer, Libra, and Capricornus, the signs auspicious for movements, journeyings, etc.; Leo, Taurus, Scorpio, and Aquila, those auspicious to stationary actions or employments ; and Gemini, Virgo, Sagittarius, and Pisces, the four auspicious to both classes.

were as yet inside. Thereupon Rajasekhara came up, had the hampers and other rubbish taken out of the cart, and began to distribute them among the poor people, who, hearing they were going away, had come to see them off. The worthy Brahmans of the neighbourhood had not, up to that moment, so much as set foot outside their doors; but no sooner did they hear it reported that Rajasekhara was giving away his furniture than up they came, running with the speed of the wind. To those who were importuning her, Manikyamba distributed the baskets and other articles which had been placed on the ground because there was no room for them in the bandy. The boxes and brass utensils were next hoisted into the cart. Articles of furniture which formerly could not be stowed in half-a-dozen bandies, were now easily packed in one—and even then left room enough for several persons to sit. Notwithstanding the fact that Rajasekhara was in such a hurry, Manikyamba went off to bid good-bye to one or two neighbouring women who were her intimate friends, and dallied away not less than two whole hours. Rajasekhara, having in the meantime had the bedsteads tied upon the top of the cart and the children snugly stowed inside, now got angry. At this Manikyamba came and took her seat in the bandy; and the lean bullocks, which had been frugally dieted on a modicum of dry straw, with as much water as they cared to drink, ever since coming into the possession of the then owner, began slowly to draw the cart. Directly at their heels walked the bandyman, who, though a perfect miser as far as feed was concerned, began to exhibit great liberality in dealing out blows. The very poor low-caste people who had so often received alms from Rajasekhara accompanied them to the outskirts of the village, where, showering blessings upon the travellers, they turned sorrowfully back. The cartman, whether from eating opium, from drinking, from natural sleepy-headedness, or from all these combined, staggered and reeled along the road until, mounting the tongue of his cart, he seated himself comfortably, and smoked a number of old half-consumed cheroots in such quick succession as to cover the sky with tiny clouds and supply those seated in the bandy with all the fragrance they could desire. Then he leaned back upon the boxes and dropped off to sleep as unconcerned as you please. The bandy barely seemed to creep, and in the meantime night fell. When, after a little, Rajasekhara peeped out, he could discover no evidence whatever that the cart was moving. Then he undertook to awaken the cartman, who was sleeping like Kumbha-karna.* Shouts had no effect whatever; and as for hitting him upon the bare feet, that only served to make the sleeper draw these appendages up, give vent to a groan, and turn over upon the other side. When with great difficulty they succeeded in rousing him, and got out to ascertain where they were, they discovered that the cart had left the road and was stuck fast in a field knee-deep in mud. All alighted, and by exerting their united strength succeeded in an hour's time in lifting the cart out of the mire and dragging it to the road. But so far were the poor bullocks from being in a fit condition to draw the cart, that it was actually necessary for some one to assist them along. So, as a return for the trouble they had taken in pulling the bandy until night, it now, being dark, fell to the lot of the riders themselves to perform that duty. All were heartily glad that this misfortune had befallen them at night rather than by day, for the clothes of the whole party were ornamented with mud flowers of all sizes and designs. Fortunately for them there were no spectators of their plight; had there been, they would have enjoyed no little sport. The cartman was a perfect Hercules, and with Rajasekhara's aid easily drew the cart. Behind came Subrahmanya leading the bullocks and women. Even had they gone

---

* The younger brother of Ravana, the sovereign of Lanka, or Ceylon, who carried off the wife of Rama. He seems to have been the sleeping Joe of the *rakshasas*, slumbering for six months of the year. His name signifies 'the pot-eared.'

afoot, they should have reached Rajahmundry in three hours; but as it was necessary for them to drag the cart into the bargain, they did not reach the house of Ramamurti, Rajasekhara's uncle's son, until twelve o'clock that night. All in the house were then fast asleep, consequently there was no one to open the door immediately on the noisy arrival of the bandy. After they had shouted awhile at the door, however, some one who lay in the porch rose and opened it. As soon as Rajasekhara's voice was heard, Ramamurti came out of the room in which he slept, embraced his brother,* and explained that they had expected them long before, and sat up waiting for them, but when nine o'clock even failed to bring them, they concluded that they had not started that day, and had taken their evening meal and just gone to rest; and what, he wanted to know, was the cause of their being so late? Giving as the reason for their tardy arrival only the explanation that their clothes and legs covered with mud to the very knee already divulged so plainly as to preclude any necessity on their part for repeating it, Rajasekhara withheld the one fact of their having drawn the bandy themselves. But when he handed the cartman the cart-hire due him, and told him to go, the fellow replied that he had had a very hard time of it, and that it was difficult to find a better pair of bullocks than his anywhere. In fine, after eulogizing his bullocks and himself at great length, he urged that he ought to receive a present. Rajasekhara, fearful that if allowed to talk longer he would divulge the fact that they had drawn the bandy, gave him a present in addition to his regular fare, and dismissed him as soon as all the things were out of the cart. Married women are prohibited from seeing others of their sex who have lost their husbands, immediately after dinner. Besides, that day was unlucky; so a widow, after first bidding all the reputable† women

---

* Cousins are, among the Hindus, regarded as brothers and sisters. This does not, however, preclude marriage alliances between them.

† Married women only are called by this term. It is considered by

go into another room and close the door, brought Rukmini in, and directing her into a separate apartment, shut the door tight. The females of the household then came out and conducted Manikyamba and the others to the west room, where, after the weeping and wailing over Rukmini's misfortune had ceased, they served up the meal that had already been prepared and kept in readiness, placing some dry-boiled rice before Rajasekhara. By the time the meal was completed it had gone three o'clock, when all retired to rest, and enjoyed a sound sleep.

Rajasekhara kept close indoors at Ramamurti's for several days. One day, however, he took the boat to Kōvūru, and there saw the place where of old Gautama did penance, and the spot where fell the fictitious cow,* bathed at the shrine Gōpada, and returned home at night. On another day he went to bathe at the Kotilinga† shrine, and there heard from a *sastri* the ancient story of Anjaneya carrying off a *linga*, and leaving it in Kasi‡—through which that city became celebrated. On

---

the Hindus a disreputable thing for any woman to be unmarried or a widow. The only unmarried women in India of marriageable age are courtesans and native Christian girls.

* 'The fictitious cow.' The story is as follows: While Gautama, the hermit god, dwelt on the south bank of the Godaveri, and did penance at the shrine Kōvūru, there came a twelve years' famine, and all the *rishis* flocked to him for refuge. Thereupon it came to pass that every day when he went out for his bath, etc., Gautama took a handful of paddy, sowed it in the sand of the Godaveri, and watered it. This, by the time he returned, was in full head, and ready to reap. On the food thus provided all the *rishis* subsisted. After the famine abated, these worthies, on taking their departure, demanded that Gautama should accompany them, and, on his refusing to comply with their request, fabricated a cow, which daily destroyed the green crop in Gautama's field. One day Gautama frightened it off with his stick, whereupon the cow and her calf fell dead. The *rishis* now charged Gautama with cow-murder (a most heinous sin in the eyes of an orthodox Hindu), and condemned him to expiate his crime by performing *chandrayana*—*i.e.*, by increasing the amount of his food one mouthful per day during the light, and diminishing it in like manner during the dark, half of the month.

† 'Linga,' a cylindrical oblong stone worshipped as the emblem of Siva. Kotilinga shrine means the shrine of 'the ten million lingas.'

‡ Kasi, the modern Benares.

yet another day he visited the fort of Rajarajanarendra,* and saw therein the spot where of old stood Chitrangi's castle, and that where Sarangadhara flew his doves. From the bystanders he heard also the story of how, of old, Amma Varu appeared to Rajarajanarendra and informed him that for whatever distance he might walk without looking back, the ground should become a fort; how, after walking straight forward for some distance, he heard a loud noise behind, and being unable longer to control his curiosity, looked back; and how a fort nearly surrounded by a gold wall immediately arose—with other tales of like nature. He then set out to visit the place where Sarangadhara's feet and hands were cut off; and, arrived at the hill, saw there beneath a lime-tree the stone slab on which the amputation was performed, observed that the whole of the surrounding landscape was bare, and entirely destitute of even so much as a blade of grass, and had a look also at the lake near by to which the *arahat* carried Sarangadhara and bathed him in its waters.

While in Rajahmundry Rajasekhara also made good use of his time in observing the habits of the people with a view to ascertaining whether there existed any diversity of manners between the townsfolk and the people who lived in the country. He began thus to acquire to a considerable degree true knowledge of the world. In that town they who displayed bracelets and rings, even though obtained by borrowing, and wore rich clothes, though brought on hire from the washerman's, were counted worthy of the highest respect. They were regarded as the most learned *pandits* who, though absolutely devoid of native ability, exhibited fine rings in their ears and wrapped huge shawls about their heads. All frequented the houses of the wealthy and eulogized their hosts as being superlatively religious and pre-eminently pious, though they had never once seen the interior of a temple in their lives, nor so much as breathed the Creator's name in their dreams.

* Rajarajanarenda, an ancient king; Chitrangi, his wife; Sarangadhara, his son. Amma Varu, the *maha sekti*, or Power of Evil.

As for genuine scholars and poets, their mouths and stomachs were always surfeited with *slokas* and verses; but, since their possessors were unable to make any external show, were seldom or never filled with food. No matter though they thrust themselves into a dozen rope-dancers' houses in a day, those who went about in scant breech-clothes, and with *juttus* knotted at the end as though they had bathed and performed their daily devotions, were eulogized for respectable men. In a word, though in secret a man committed a *lac* of evil deeds, granted only that he was irreproachable in the one point of external hypocrisy—those who were fully cognizant of the baseness of his conduct treated him, even in company, with greater politeness than they showed those who were of spotless reputation. How abominable soever their conduct was as regards righteousness, in the one matter of creed at least they were outwardly most pious. Individuals who were unable to build even so much as a wretched hut for a bosom friend who was suffering for want of standing shelter, expended thousands in the construction of temples for the use of stone images. Rajasekhara counted no less than one hundred and twenty-three temples which had fallen into ruins because deprived of incomes by the death of the builders; and then surmised that probably as many as ten million *lingas* into the bargain lay buried in the debris of temples which at some time in the past had crumbled to dust in this way. Except harlots, not a woman in the place could read a word. The education such women obtained served only to increase adultery, entangle men in their net, and bring ruin upon the town; but assisted not a whit the increase of learning, or correction of immorality.

Rajasekhara had proposed remaining there until the 7th, and then starting for Benares; but Ramamurti importuned him so strongly to tarry until the New Year that he could not refuse. In the month Palgu, on the day of new moon, there occurred a total eclipse of the sun. At the moment of seizure all the people bathed in the Godaveri, and poured out libations* to their ancestors. Some, for merit, offered prayers to the nine planets, and made gifts of the nine kinds of grain† to Brahmans. A number of ritualists and old women began to wail with tears that it was all over with the sun. Those who considered themselves the wisest of this lot repeated *mantras* to drive away the demon that had seized upon the sun. Others, wiser even than these, knowing that it was a sin to have undigested food in the stomach at the time of an eclipse, fasted for at least nine hours before that event. All put *darbha*-grass in such dishes as contained food. The older ones, thinking that if pregnant women appeared out of doors on such an occasion they would give birth to deformed children, locked such females up in a room and bade them not stir hand or foot. Others again, obtaining possession of *mantras* by feeing those who called themselves *mantricians*, were repeating their orisons in water breast-deep in order the more easily to succeed in their object. Some simpletons who supposed herbs to possess peculiar efficacy at the time of an eclipse, were waving lamps and incense to the trees, and pulling roots, stark naked, and with *juttus* flowing. Holy Brahmans, asserting that charity performed at such a time was specially meritorious, stood in the stream knee-deep with cloths tied up so as not to get them wet, and bestowed water-alms upon fools and women.

Rajasekhara also bathed in accordance with the ancient custom; but he considered all who performed such acts as the above mere fools, and entered into a discussion with the *pandits* of the place on the subject of eclipses. While he held to his belief in the Jyotisastra,‡ he discredited the *puranas* only when these

---

* Of water poured from the hand.

† The nine kinds of grain proper to be presented with burnt offerings, oblations, etc., and to the gods and nine planets, one to each: (1) wheat, to the sun; (2) paddy, to the moon; (3) a kind of lentil, to Mars; (4) pulse, to Mercury; (5) Bengal gram, to Jupiter; (6) beans, to Venus; (7) sesamum, to Saturn; (8) a kind of pulse—*Phaseolus mungo*—to Rahu; (9) gram, to Ketu.

‡ The Hindu astronomy, the two principal treatises of which are named below.

were directly antagonistic to it. Quoting that *sloka* from the Sidhanta-Siromani, which says, '*The moon, moving like a cloud in a lower sphere, overtakes the sun (by reason of its quicker motion), and obscures its shining disc by its own dark body;*' and that from the Surya-Sidhanta, which says, '*The moon being like a cloud in a lower sphere covers the sun (in a solar eclipse); but in a lunar one the moon, moving eastward, enters the earth's shadow, and (therefore) the shadow obscures her disc,*'*—he argued at great length that when the sun is above the earth, granted the moon, owing to its higher rate of speed, to come between in a line with these two bodies, an eclipse of the sun must occur, and that this phenomenon is not caused by Rahu † swallowing it; that if what the *puranists* asserted were the cause of eclipses, we should be powerless to ascertain the intentions of Rahu and Ketu, and so could not foretell the time of an eclipse; that there would then be no reason in solar eclipses occurring at the time of new, and lunar eclipses at that of full moon only; that everyone knew that Rahu and Ketu had never appeared in the heavens; and, were they really of such size as to admit of their swallowing the sun and moon, how was it they never showed themselves at the time of an eclipse? and even granting that Rahu swallowed the sun or moon, there was no satisfactory reason for an eclipse being visible in one country and not in another, as the *panchanga* showed was the case. No suitable answer to these arguments suggested itself to any of the *pandits* present; nevertheless, they shouted tremendously. As for the spectators, they understood not a word of the discussion,

---

* Translation of Asiatic Society of Bengal from the Sanskrit.

† Rahu, the moon's ascending node, regarded by the Hindus as one of the nine planets, in the form of a monstrous serpent or dragon. Ketu, the moon's descending node, or *cauda draconis*, the red serpent into which the trunk of Asura Sainhikeya, severed from the head (Rahu, *caput draconis*, as above) at the churning of the sea of milk, was changed, and which, with Rahu, is said to swallow the sun and moon for betraying them.

and, in consequence, applauded as best men those who bore the title *sastri*, because they brayed the loudest, and sneered at Rajasekhara's arguments as Buddhistical. Than the pleasure necessarily consequent on jeering at another, they possessed no higher enjoyment; so the choicest of this lot of ignoramuses, who knew not even so much as the smell of learning, made all sorts of sport of Rajasekhara, and enjoyed to the utmost all the amusement they could derive from the occasion.

In the meantime the termination of the eclipse approached, and all rushed to take the release-bath. The females, after bathing, had gone on ahead and done the cooking; so, when all danger to the sun was quite past, the others followed suit, and ate their first meal that day by lamp-light.

CHAPTER VIII.

The New Year—Rajasekhara's Journey—A Rajah is Sunstruck in the Vicinity of Rajanagara—They meet a *Yogi* near the Black Lake — And are attacked by Highwaymen—Rukmini's Death.

AFTER daylight on New Year's day * Ramamurti called a barber and had him anoint Rajasekhara and Subrahmanya. The anointing and bathing of the male members of the household at an end, all the females followed suit. Then all, in accordance with the national custom, partook of margosa flowers and bits of green mango with sauce of fresh tamarinds, dined at mid-day on pastries, and observed the day as a feast-day. Instead of getting all the enjoyment possible out of a holiday, as they should do, the people of this country dine at a late hour, and harass their bodies more severely than at other times. After the mid-day heat had somewhat abated Ramamurti took Rajasekhara along and proceeded to the temple of Venugopalaswami to hear the new *panchanga* read. Already the astrologer had placed before him in a platter some unbroken rice coloured

* In the month Chetra, April—May.

with saffron, and, as they entered, was reading the *sloka*: '*Worthy of audience is the estimable panchanga, the bestower of universal blessing on mortals, the destroyer of enemies, the deliverer from the guilt of evil dreams, the conferrer of benefit equal to that accruing from a bath in Ganga or the gift of a cow, the prolonger of life, the most excellent, the most pure, the giver of offspring and joy and wealth, the most potent factor in the performance of any deed.*' He expatiated on the perfection of the *Samkranti* personage,* announced the outcome of the year, foretold the increase or decrease of paddy and other crops, of scorpions and other venomous reptiles; and when the people did not know their natal, ascertained their nominal stars, and revealed to them the numbers of their *kandayas* † and their gains and losses for the coming year. The ryots and others present took wise precautions against the presence of cyphers in their *kandayas* by slipping something into the astrologer's hand.

'Astrologer,' said Ramamurti after the reading of the *panchanga*, 'how many years have elapsed from the commencement of the Kaliyuga ‡ to the present time?'

'It is now,' replied the astrologer '4719 years since the commencement of the Kaliyuga, 1541 from that of the Salivahana era, and 1676 of the Vikramarkian.'§

'From the signs of the times,' asked Ramamurti, 'can you tell how much longer our country is to continue under the dominion of barbarians?'

* *i.e.*, the Sun.

† The year is divided into three astrological periods of four months each, called *kandayas*. Each month of each *kandaya* is associated with one of the twenty-seven lunar mansions, and is productive of gain or loss according as the influence of the asterism is good or evil. The months and asterisms corresponding to them are represented by numbers determined by means of the *panchanga*. Even numbers denote full, odd numbers half, profits; cyphers denote loss.

‡ Hindu chronology divides all time into four ages or *yugas*—the Krita, Treta, Dvapara, and Kali. These comprise 1,728,000, 1,296,000, 864,000, and 432,000 years respectively, and correspond to the golden, silver, brazen, and iron ages. Brown defines the Kaliyuga as 'modern times beginning from the deluge.'

§ 1618-19 A.D., the date of our story.

'The rule of the Mohammedans will be supreme in the land for five hundred years,' replied the astrologer; 'then there will arise a ruler of the lineage of Pusapati with a tail the size of a margosa berry.* He will conquer the whole earth from Ramnad to the Himalayas.'

It being now evening, they tied up the *panchanga* and proceeded to their homes.

Rajasekhara had decided to set out on his pilgrimage to Kasi on the 2nd; and, in spite of the repeated remonstrances of the whole household, had in Piduparti Ramasastri, the astrologer who had read the *panchanga* in the temple, to fix a time for the journey. After a careful scrutiny of the date and diurnal stars, he decided that nine seconds past eight o'clock that very night was a favourable time at which to set out on the pilgrimage. Thinking the hour an undesirable one for commencing a journey with one's family, Rajasekhara placed a cloth, in which was wrapped a book, in a neighbouring house, postponed their exodus, and determined to start as soon as it was day. Seeing Ramamurti about to send a message for a bandy, he declared that that would never do; for, should they go by bandy, no merit would accrue from the pilgrimage. He thereupon declared his purpose to go afoot. That night Ramamurti presented them all with new cloths; and, rising just at break of day, ere the others were astir, held himself in readiness against the time of their setting out. Charging him to keep them safely until their return, Rajasekhara handed over to him the utensils, bedsteads, and clothes-boxes which he had brought from Dhavalesvaram, retaining only such articles as they would have special need of on the way. When Manikyamba and the others were about to depart, Ramamurti's wife accompanied them as far as the street, where, recollecting that they were undertaking a journey to a far country, she began to weep. After taking leave of all at the door they waited for a single Brahman who was coming up the street to pass, and, perceiving a married

* The family title and tradition of the Maharajahs of Vizianagram.

woman approaching just beyond, took the road on the strength of this good omen,* and began their long walk. Ramamurti saw them to the outskirts of the village, where, after cautioning them that they were going a long journey and must proceed cannily, he turned back and went home. Rajasekhara, pointing out to his wife and children the trees and other objects of interest by the roadside, went his way with a light heart.

'Do you see,' said he, 'how yon *marri*-tree is covered with buds from top to bottom, and how charming it looks with its clusters of coral-red berries?'

'Yes, yes,' replied Subrahmanya, 'but the young mango just at its foot is more wonderful in its mauve silk dress of newly-expanded leaves. And see! on the tip-top branch sits a black cuckoo, ravishing the ear with its melodious note!'

'Papa,' cried Rukmini, 'do look how that beautiful parrot is swinging head downwards from a branch and pecking a green guava to bits with its beak.'

'Oh, brother, won't you get that green mango for me?' chimed in Sita.

'There are half-ripe ones under the tree that the parrots have knocked off; take one of them, dear.'

Away danced Sita and brought four or five of the unripe mangoes, which, on biting and trying, she declared—cracking her armpits by way of emphasis—were as sweet as sugar.

'I just had a whiff of jasmine blossoms from somewhere,' said Manikyamba.

At that moment Subrahmanya shouted, 'Oh, mother, come quick! Look, there is a wild jasmine growing on that *pogada*-tree. It's covered with basketfuls of white blossoms! Water it as often as we like, the jasmine we have at home never blooms like this.'

---

* Some auguries favourable to a journey are: music of kettledrum or conch, good wishes, ripe and green fruit, flowers, a married woman, a dancing woman, a virgin, white boiled rice, an elephant, a bull, milk, curds, fish, a toddy *karadi*, saffron.

'And how sweet the scent of the *pogada* blossoms is, too,' said Manikyamba.

'And though the sun is now five hours high,' observed Subrahmanya, 'how cool the wind blows! Do we ever have the wind so cool as this at home in summer?'

'How incapable we are,' moralized Rajasekhara, 'of appreciating and adoring the greatness of God, who, with unmerited kindness, has created such beautiful things to afford delight to every sense, and bestowed them for the free enjoyment and happiness of travellers! When we constantly remained close at home, we knew nothing whatever of such delights as these; and yet we piqued ourselves on being happier than all the rest of the world. How fortunate are the uncivilized wanderers of the wilderness who, living their whole lives amid such scenes, enjoy pleasures which have as their source the goodness of that Great Spirit who is kinsman to the lowly! Ah, truly we never found the summer so agreeable as this in town!'

'Mamma,' interrupted Sita, 'I can't walk any farther. Take me up.'

'Come on as far as those trees—I'll take you up then. Rukmini, why are you falling behind? Walk a little faster,' cried Manikyamba.

'I'm not accustomed to it, and my feet are blistered. I'm not able to walk a step faster,' replied she.

'I asked a herdsman, and he said it was but a couple of miles to the next village. It is now nearly mid-day. You must do your best to walk a little faster somehow or other,' said Rajasekhara.

'I'm carrying Sita,' replied Manikyamba; 'she's crying of hunger. At a little distance there on the right-hand side I hear a sound like men's voices. Perhaps it's a village. Shall we stop there till afternoon?'

'There are some men running in a great hurry,' replied Rajasekhara; 'maybe some accident has happened to one of their number. Come, let us go faster.'

They increased their pace and soon neared the spot

from which the shouts proceeded. All at once several persons burst out of a close-packed crowd of men at a little distance to the south of the highway, and came running towards them shouting, 'Some buttermilk to purify it!' Rajasekhara stopped and asked them what the noise was about. One of the number, a shepherd, replied that 'A Rajah had fainted under a *ravi*-tree from sunstroke.'

'Couldn't you pour a little water down his throat?' asked Rajasekhara.

'At first we were agoing to give him water; but we're Sudras, and so the Rajah refused it because he said he wouldn't take water from us to drink. But he wasn't able to stand the terrible thirst, and soon consented to drink the water. But just then the leader of our crowd came up, and said that if we poured water into the mouth of a Rajah 'twould be committing a sin, and sent us to bring some buttermilk to purify the water. Our village is about half a mile from here. You look like Brahmans; if you have any good water by you, go quick and pour a few drops down his throat and get the merit yourselves.'

As soon as Rajasekhara heard these words he seized the vessel of drinking-water which Rukmini had in her hand, and running to the tree made his way into the midst of the group. Here he found a man lying upon the bare ground in the shade of the tree, pointing to his mouth and making signs for water with his hand. 'The Rajah's dying from sheer obstinacy. I don't care what harm it does, I'll give him some water and save his life,' one of the crowd was saying as he drew near with a wooden drinking-cup in his hand. But an old man interposed: 'We're now living the life of Sudras for the very reason that heretofore in a former birth we committed, it's hard to say how many, sins of this sort; and must you commit the additional sin of making this Rajah here an outcast? Take my advice and don't give him the water,' remonstrated he, seizing upon and staying the other's hand. By this time the Rajah's eyes were rolling wildly, and with an attempt to raise his hand to his mouth he fell prostrate in a convulsion. Rajasekhara at once went to him and first moistened his parched lips with the water, and then poured a small quantity into his mouth, which after a few moments the sufferer began to swallow feebly. Rajasekhara then took some water in his hand and dashed it in his face; and, after swallowing a little more, the prostrate man opened his eyes and looked around, and turned over on his other side. After lying in this position for a short time he sat up much revived, and lavished many *namaskaras** of deep gratitude upon Rajasekhara for saving his life. The men who had run to the village now returned with some fruit and buttermilk, which they gave him. After disposing of the fruit and taking a drink† he felt better, and all the bystanders took their departure. In the meantime Manikyamba and her companions had been sitting in the shade of a tree alleviating in some degree the weariness resulting from their long walk. Rajasekhara was very much exhausted, but hearing there was not a single village in the vicinity, he determined to get to Rajanagara somehow or other that day, and directing all the members of his family to rise, he again took the road, conversing with the Rajah.

'Rajah, what is your name? Where is your place of residence? And how did you come here alone?'

'My name,' replied his companion, 'is Ramarajah; our place of residence is Kattamuru in the vicinity of Peddapuram. We have four yoke‡ of land under cultivation there. I went some ten days ago to see our relatives, who live in Rajahmundry, and yesterday at daybreak set out on my return; but as I was coming along an enormous tiger suddenly confronted me in the road. Wrapping my thick mantle about my left arm as

---

* An obeisance made by bowing to the earth with joined hands.

† Caste rules forbid a high-caste man taking water from the hands of a low-caste man. But he may take fruit and buttermilk without committing a misdemeanour.

‡ A bovate or yoke of land is that quantity of land which may be worked with a single yoke of oxen or bullocks.

quickly as I could, I thrust it into the tiger's mouth and stabbed the brute with the knife in my right hand. The tiger was of immense strength, so without paying the least attention to my thrust, he dragged me a long distance into the jungle, flooding his whole path with streams of blood. In the meantime I hadn't been idle, but continued to stab him again and again with my knife, until the beast, unable to walk farther, fell to the ground beneath a tree. I dropped the knife from my right hand, and at last succeeded in forcing open its jaws and freeing my left arm. Just then a royal tiger, more powerful than the first one, leapt upon me from a thicket close at hand. By the blessing of God, however, it missed its aim a little and tumbled into a small pit at my side. As there was no time to secure my knife, I at once crawled up the tree, and by the time the tiger was ready for another spring, reached the top branch, where I perched. That tiger, do you know, never budged an inch, but took his seat and sat down directly beneath the tree. There he stayed until full ten o'clock this morning, when he at last got tired and moved off. I had been on the branch of that tree from early morning yesterday without sleep or food; so the moment the tiger was gone I crept softly down, secured my knife, and set out with it in my hand. All day yesterday I suffered terrible torture from the sun. My tongue clung to my mouth, and my legs lost all power of motion. But in some way I managed to drag my body along to this tree, where I fell. See, I have two wounds on my arm alone,' said he, baring that member. Then he drew forth from a sheath resembling a walking staff a knife, which he exhibited. This Rajasekhara took and examined with many exclamations of astonishment at the daring deed he had performed.

'You have to-day,' proceeded Ramarajah, 'restored to me the life I lost. Though I should lay down that life for you, it would not free me from the obligation I am under to you for the service you have rendered me.

Please be so good as to receive my *namaskaras* as an expression of my heartfelt thankfulness. How deeply I regret that while Fortune enables others to show their gratitude in gifts of money and by like acts, she forces me, who am at present poor, to express mine by mere empty words—and that, too, to so great a benefactor as yourself! But should you ever stand in need of any kindness that lies in my power to show, I am ready to do it—and that, too, without regard even for my life. Where do you go now?'

'We are off on a pilgrimage to Kasi.'

'This hot season is not at all a good time for so long a journey. You will certainly be sunstruck by the way in this heat. Besides, the whole road is infested with robbers. Have you any relatives in Rajahmundry? Or perhaps that is where you live?'

'Do you know Koteti Ramamurti? He is my uncle's son—it was after a fifteen days' stay at his house that I set out. Our native place is Dhavalesvaram.'

'What is your name, and what are all these to you?'

'My name is Rajasekhara; he is my son; these two girls are my daughters, while she is my wife.'

'What's your reason for starting on a pilgrimage in such hot weather as this? From your manner I should take you to be people who have enjoyed considerable prosperity.'

'I was once a wealthy man, it is true; but I squandered all the wealth I possessed in gratuities at my daughter's wedding, and in gifts to knaves who plied their flatteries to my face—became thus reduced to poverty, and at length set out on this pilgrimage. I always swallowed their flatteries and was satisfied; they swallowed my money and were more than satisfied. At last a *byragi*, on the pretence of converting it into gold, absconded with all my gold and silver—leaving me only so much ashes—and made me a beggar in very truth.'

'You are not people who were ever in the habit of making journeys to distant countries before. Take my advice and tarry in Bhimavaram, at least until summer is over. That is a great and justly celebrated shrine. Near the Bhima river stands the temple of Bhimesvaraswami. The town is only two miles distant from Peddapuram. Krishna Gajapati Maharajah, who rules Peddapuram, is immensely rich; he goes about incognito devising means for bettering the condition of his people. A relative of ours has a capital situation with him. Were you in Bhimavaram, I'd speak a word to him and get you a situation when a chance offered.'

Rajasekhara was a good fellow; so he said for the present that he would consider the matter after reaching Peddapuram. But in view of his would-be benefactor's then condition he did not entertain the least hope that he could secure him a position. By the time this conversation came to an end, they were near the village.

'How far is the village from those trees?' asked Rajasekhara.

'We are quite near the village. Those trees are on the bank of the tank. The choultry is directly opposite the tank.'

'Won't you take dinner with us to-day?'

'I have relatives in the village; I shall go there for my meal, and come slowly on in the cool of the evening. You have women along; so you had better be off just as soon as you've had dinner, and pass Vedimangala before the day closes. That's a great place for highwaymen. Try hard to get to Peddapuram somehow before it gets dark, and stay there a day. I'm quite used up, and for that reason can't come with you now; but I'll catch you up to-morrow;' and with that Ramarajah saluted Rajasekhara, and taking leave of all, and charging them to be careful in the road, went his way.

After cooking and eating their meal they set out once more, and with bodies completely drenched with sweat, drinking water by the pint at every few paces, and resting now and then in the shade of the trees, they dragged along as though every step were an *amada*,* and at

* An *amada* equals eight miles.

length, while there was still three hours' daylight, arrived at the Black Lake. Here, at the roots of a *juvvi*-tree growing just below the bund of the tank, stood a booth of palmira leaves, and in it sat a *yogi*—his whole body smeared over with sacred ashes, and *rudraksha* rosaries about his neck, head, and arms—who with his hand signalled them to approach, and bade them be seated on a mat near by. Twirling in his right hand a rosary of *tulasi* beads, he began mumbling his mantras and asking occasional questions between whiles.

'Travellers, you are very warm and exhausted with your hard journey. Tarry here a little and rest. It seems you have your family along. Where do you go?'

'We are going on a pilgrimage to Kasi,' replied Rajasekhara.

'Pilgrimage to so distant a country is impracticable except for the wealthy. There are no choultries on the way. Did you not lay by any money against your start?'

'Where should such poor people as we get much money? We have, however, brought a hundred rupees in cash. We propose to manage the pilgrimage to Kasi and return on that amount in some way.'

'You must exercise great caution. At a distance of four miles from here, near Vedimangala, robbers attack wayfarers. If you will but wait a little, I'll send along some of my disciples as company for you,' said the *yogi*, again beginning to tell his beads and mumble his orisons.

As, however, his disciples were very slow in coming, Rajasekhara became disturbed in mind. The day also was fast declining.

'Swami,' ventured he, 'your people haven't arrived yet. It wants but two hours of sundown. Will you send a messenger quickly?'

'Certainly I will,' replied the *yogi*; and rising briskly he went to a hut which stood at a distance of a hundred yards from the *juvvi*-tree and called out, 'Gopaliga!' From within there crept a hillsman wrapped in a ragged cloth. He was the possessor of a pug nose, high forehead, bushy head, and irregular teeth, united to a body as black as coal. The *yogi* conversed with him for a moment on some subject, and brought him over to the booth, where, in the hearing of Rajasekhara, he sent him off with the order, 'Call our men to accompany these people in case they should need assistance.'

'Swami,' said Rajasekhara, 'it's hard to say when your disciples will come. We must pass Vedimangala before night falls. Shall we go on?'

'Ah, what you say is very true. Do you walk along; they'll come and join you at once.'

Rajasekhara delayed no longer, but started with his wife and children. Often he felt the bundle upon his shoulder, and his heart went pit-a-pat whenever the thought of robbers came into his head. If a cricket but chirped he looked back, and started in terror at the slightest movement of the bushes at the roadside.

The hillsman who had been despatched by the *yogi* quickly outwalked them, and, taking a copious drink of toddy somewhere on the road, reached the rendezvous by dint of much staggering and stumbling and rolling of eyes that were like live coals. 'Hallo you!' cried he, striking with his hand a man who lay asleep in a hovel there, and arousing him; 'a Brahman, his wife, son, and two daughters are coming with a hundred rupees, and our chief says you're to go as quick as you can to the ant tamarind-tree.' This message delivered, he went away. On hearing these words the other spent a moment in cogitation, and then rose right gladly. Being well acquainted with the paths and rendezvous, he took his knife in his hand and left the hut without a word. The hillsman made a cross cut, spoke a word with another man whom he met in the way, and again joined the *yogi*. At his order he slung a bow and arrows over his shoulder, and set out on a run to deflect the wayfarers from the road, and guide them to the vicinity of the ant tamarind-tree. When he joined them it was just dusk.

'As the other disciples didn't come, the *yogi* sent me, sir, for your protection,' said he, addressing Rajasekhara. 'I've caught up with you just in the nick of time. We're near the spot where the highwaymen usually make their attack; but you needn't be at all afraid. We'll just leave this road and take a footpath; then when we've passed the place where there's the most danger, we'll get into the highway again.

'Yours is the responsibility of getting us safely through in some way. We'll come whatever way you bid us.'

Turning aside from the main road, the hillsman conducted them along a narrow path. The sky had now become overcast, and they were soon wrapped in such dense darkness that they could not see the road. The chirping of the birds upon the trees had ceased; nothing was on the wing but a few owls and other night birds in quest of prey. The grave-cricket sent up its creaking note on every hand. The roaring of wild beasts and the hissing of serpents fell with terrible distinctness on their ears. Now and then lightning gleamed spasmodically from the clouds and illumined the path for a moment. After they had walked a short distance in this manner, a light appeared in the distance, which, as they gradually approached it, shaped itself into a huge fire beneath an immense tamarind-tree. While walking thus in the darkness Rajasekhara's life was not in his body, while the others dragged their limbs along with their lives in their hands. All resolved that should they escape from the dangers of that night and reach even the meanest village alive, they would never again travel afoot. Manikyamba vowed a sacrifice of a male buffalo to the local goddess on reaching the village. They proceeded thus with faltering steps until they reached a clearing, when two figures rose from before the fire where they were seated and came towards them. Their bodies were closely wrapped in blankets; cheroots were stuck in their mouths; and on the shoulder of each rested a huge club. No sooner did they see these apparitions than the travellers became rooted to the spot in helpless terror. The hillsman, who was in the rear, shouted 'Robbers!' and, the last of the group, was the first to beat a retreat. One of the highwaymen now strode forward, lifted his club in both hands, and without a word brought it down with all his might upon the head of Rukmini, who happened to be in front. Beneath this blow she fell to the earth insensible, like a plantain-tree lopped off at the roots. At that moment some one drew his sword with a cry of 'Back! back!' and falling upon the scoundrels like lightning smote one of them on the skull. At the stroke the head flew off like a melon and rolled to a distance, while the decapitated trunk sank upon the earth with arms and legs threshing convulsively, the blood spouting in streams as though ejected from a squirt-gun. Seeing his opponent armed, himself alone, and two other males among the travellers, the second highwayman bolted with the hillsman as fast as his legs could carry him. The brave fellow followed them a short distance, sword in hand; but as they had passed out of sight in an instant, he soon returned and rejoined Rajasekhara.

'Rajasekhara! How many times did I not tell you at noon that you must pass this spot while it was still light? You brought this danger on yourselves by disregarding my advice.'

'Oh, ho! Is it Ramarajah? You came to our assistance and saved our lives like a patron saint. Had you delayed another instant we should all have been in the power of those villains. But how did you manage to get here at this time of night?'

'The hillsman who came with you was sent by the *yogi* to summon the gang. Unable to walk in the sun I was lying down in a hut, when he, mistaking me for one of their number, said that their chief had ordered me to be off to this tamarind-tree to plunder some Brahmans. When I heard that I guessed those Brahmans to be no other than you. I didn't let the grass

'The hillsman shouted "Robbers," and beat a retreat' (p. 108).

grow under my feet then, but hurried to the place
where the *yogi* stays, with the intention of heading off
the robbers. There I learned that the scoundrels had
already come and talked with the *yogi* and gone away.
My heart was in my mouth lest any danger should
befall you ere I could arrive, so without any thought of
weariness I came on at a run and managed to join you
just at the right moment—and right glad I am that my
life has at last proved good for something.'

While Ramarajah was talking, Manikyamba had felt
Rukmini over from head to foot and now began to wail
vociferously. Both Ramarajah and Rajasekhara now
approached and examined the insensible girl's heart
and put their fingers to her nostrils; but, unable to
discover any traces of respiration, they came to the
sorrowful conclusion that she had died from the effects
of the blow and from fright. Ramarajah also felt her
pulse and ascertained for certain that she had expired.
Then they all gathered about the corpse and wailed.
Just at that moment the roar of a tiger was heard
close at hand. While all, even in the midst of their
great affliction, were trembling at the sound, Ramarajah
cheered them with words of encouragement and attempted to persuade them that it was unsafe to remain
there in the very heart of a jungle infested with wild
beasts, and hinted that they could return after daylight
and perform the burning of the corpse and other ceremonies. But they, unwilling to abandon their darling
in the dense jungle, paid no attention to his words, but
wept at the recollection of Rukmini's lovable qualities.
Just then the tiger gave a nearer and more frightful
roar. At this all their courage melted away like dew
before the rays of the sun. Then, in accordance with
Ramarajah's sensible admonition, they reluctantly left
Rukmini—how hard it was!—and, looking back every
few steps, at length followed their guide aimlessly to Peddapuram. How natural for mortals, when their own lives
are in jeopardy, to forget the peril of those they love more
than life itself, in order to escape from personal danger!

CHAPTER IX.

Rajasekhara reaches Peddapuram—His Grief at the Loss of Rukmini's Body—Occurrences in Peddapuram—He proceeds to Bhimavaram—Events there—He sends Subrahmanya to Pitapuram.

The same night Ramarajah, having slowly conducted Rajasekhara and his family to Peddapuram, set them down at the choultry near the Tirupati Rajah's tank, and went his way, after prevailing upon them by dint of much persuasion to consent to abandon the Kasi pilgrimage and stop in Bhimavaram. On considering the events of but a single night's journey—the loss of their daughter, they, though escaped with their lives, with swollen feet and in such wretched plight as to be unable to put one foot before the other—Rajasekhara trembled at the very name of pilgrimage, and decided upon spending a few days in Bhimavaram and seeing the Rajah when opportunity offered. Through grief at the loss of Rukmini and fatigue consequent on travel, they cooked and ate nothing that night. Sleep visited the eyes of none of their number. After dragging out the night as though it were an age, Rajasekhara rose with the crowing of the cock, and set out alone down the Vedimangala road to look for Rukmini's body. After proceeding for quite a distance he inquired the way of a shepherd boy, and, entering the jungle, at length reached the spot where the robbers had attacked them, by the time the sun was two hours high. No trace, however, of Rukmini's body could he find there, except a few drops of blood on the sand. Wild with grief, he sought her again and again in every direction, and finding no vestige of her anywhere, returned as often to the place from which he had started. After sitting here for a while upon the green sward and watering the grass with his tears, he arrived at the conclusion that some wild beast had made away with the body of his child. Perplexity as to how he was to carry home these sad tidings and make them known to his wife and children, augmented his grief. Slowly rising, he left the place with faltering footsteps, weeping all the way and recalling Rukmini's virtues. By midday he succeeded in dragging his body to the house, where he sank exhausted on the doormat. He attempted to speak, but the words refused to come; and moistening his parched lips with his tongue he remained silent. Manikyamba flew into the house and brought a *chembu* of cold water, which she put to his lips, wiping away the sweat from his face with the end of her cloth, and fanning him gently. After she had thus alleviated somewhat her husband's extreme exhaustion, he felt relieved, and told them in few and faltering words, and with copious tears and many efforts to swallow his grief, the sad news of Rukmini's disappearance. Immediately the whole family fell to wailing most obstreperously. The *choultry* Brahman and the bystanders heard the noise and ran in to ascertain what the matter was; and on learning the calamity that had befallen them, offered many consolations and carried them off to dinner. They seated themselves by the leafen plates, but the grains of rice which they attempted to swallow refused to go down; and after remaining seated a moment they left the meal and retired sorrowful. Just as they were washing their hands in the well inclosure, the cries of men running up the street fell upon their ears. On going into the street to see what the uproar meant, they saw at some distance to the east a huge blaze and clouds of smoke shooting up into the sky. At that moment the *choultry* Brahman came up and said the potters' street was on fire, and called to Rajasekhara to come and see the fun. Though a kind-hearted man enough, Rajasekhara was just then overwhelmed by a mountain of sorrow, and feeling indisposed to leave the house he made no reply. Subrahmanya, on the other hand, was a mere lad who had never before known what it was to suffer affliction; so no sooner did he hear that others were in distress than he straightway forgot his own sorrow and started off after the Brahman with the intention of rendering any assistance that lay in his power. By the time they reached the spot the populace had gathered in thousands and were watching the sight; but not a single person was attempting to extinguish the fire. The bamboo poles upon the houses cracked at the joints and exploded with a report like that of artillery. Dry palmira leaves rose upon the breeze like sky-rockets. The tank in the vicinity had gone dry from the heat of the sun, and, this being empty, the water in such wells as still held out had retreated to the nether world and afforded no facilities even for dipping it up with buckets; consequently the proprietors of the burning houses, unable to obtain water, set to work to tear up the roofs. The owners of adjoining houses, however, fearing that if they lifted even so much as the palmira thatch upon their dwellings, they would necessarily have the trouble of replacing it again, neglected this precaution, and mounted and remained perched upon the ridge-pole with pots of water in their hands—refused and hidden when the owners of the burning buildings came and begged for it—until their own houses caught, when they dropped the water-pots on the spot and descended with loud lamentations. Still others, through fear that the furniture in their houses would be burned, carried it out and deposited it in the street. While, after leaving one article, they were gone for another, some magnanimous experts in deeds of neighbourly kindness would—when no one was looking—appropriate the articles thrown down in the street, and insure their safety by hiding them carefully in their own houses.

While the potters' quarter was thus falling a prey to the greed of Parasu Rama,* the *choultry* Brahman took Subrahmanya to the shade of a tree at some little distance and began to gossip about the burning of the houses.

'Do you know,' queried he, 'the cause of the houses burning down at midday in this way?'

* The Hindu Vulcan, to whose agency fires are ascribed.

The potters' street on fire (p. 114).

'These are thatched houses,' replied Subrahmanya, 'and so they may have caught fire accidentally from the potteries and burned down. Or perhaps some one had a grudge and set the houses on fire.'

'Neither of the reasons you give is the correct one. An evil spirit has just come to the village and set it on fire in this way—make up your mind to that.'

'Why, you came here with me this very moment, didn't you? How can you say for certain, without first inquiring of anyone, that an evil spirit set fire to the houses?'

'Don't I know the affairs of my own village? It burns down half a dozen times every year in the summer. Each time, the villagers make a feast to the goblin and send it away. If it isn't caused by a goblin as I say, why don't it catch fire in the rainy season?'

'If the burning of the houses really be the work of a goblin, what's the reason it returns again when you have once made it a feast and dismissed it? In the rainy season the thatch of the houses is soaked with rain, and so——'

'I know neither the rhyme nor the reason of the thing. The mere mention of reasons always gives me a headache. So be assured that what I say is the truth, and don't contradict it. But even if you don't believe me now, you will to-morrow, at all events, when you see the *tamasa* with your own eyes.'

While this conversation was going on, the fire-fiend, aided by his mate the wind-god, had completely consumed the potters' quarter, and, satisfied, retired to rest. While the owners of the burnt houses and the losers of the stolen goods were smarting under their loss, some of the spectators actually went away rejoicing that they had found a live coal of sufficient size to light their cheroots, and that coals would be cheap on the morrow. Just behind them Subrahmanya and the Brahman walked back to the *choultry*.

A Brahman who was on his way to the village of Rukmini's mother-in-law happening into the *choultry* for his meal in the meanwhile, Rajasekhara had written a letter detailing her untimely death and given it into his hands to deliver to his daughter's mother-in-law in order that the requisite obsequies might be attended to with all despatch.

The day following, Rajasekhara was sitting upon the street *pial* after his midday meal, when a number of people came that way to the roll of drums and tom-toms, shouting loudly and drinking from a pot which they had placed upon a cart. Behind them again trooped a large mob who, dividing into groups, beat with sticks the low roofs of the houses along the road. The *choultry* Brahman burst from this group with a single cloth bound tightly about his waist, a stout stick in his hand, and his whole body streaming with sweat, seized Subrahmanya's hand, and dragged him down, crying, 'Yesterday when I told you, you said it was false, didn't you? Now, at least, you'll believe, won't you?'

'Hold on,' expostulated Subrahmanya; 'I'll come. What procession is this?'

'Didn't I tell you yesterday? When the goblin that burns the houses comes to the village, this is how they do. Did you see him who was walking in front with the *margosa*-branch in one hand and a cane in the other?'

'He who had the big rouge *bottu* on? Yes, I saw him. Who is he?'

'He's the identical *mantrician* who's managing this business. It won't take him long to expel the goddess that's been burning the houses lately. His name's Viradass.'

'What has he already done?'

'First he begged two handfuls of rice at each of seven houses, had a new pot brought, and made a fire in the middle of the street. Into the pot he threw the rice he had collected, added to it some *munuga* greens and oil-cake, and boiled the whole for a watch and a half. Then he removed the pot and set it on the ground while he cleaned the middle of the street with dung, and drew in lines of red, white, black, green, and leaf-juice, a picture of Bhaitalu. Next he drew the magic diagram of Bhaitalu, made *puja*, burnt incense, and offered lamps and fruit. Then after emptying the pot upon seven platters—each one was made of seven leaves of trees sewed together—he planted a stake in the middle of the street and tied to it the Bhaitalu diagram, and the command he had written to the demon, and did everything else that is usually deemed essential. Then we hoisted the pot upon the cart, and are now parading the town belabouring the houses with these sticks. Presently we'll go to the temple of the village goddess, after which there'll be something wonderful take place.'

'If that's the case, I'll come along too,' said Subrahmanya, starting off with him.

When the crowd reached the temple of the local goddess, the *mantrician* read in a loud voice the mandate which he had penned to the village goddess as follows :

'The mandate of Viradass *mantrician*, to Maridi Maha Lakshmi, patron goddess of Peddapuram — Whereas some evil spirit has entered this place and is burning the houses, you, being goddess of the village, have no business to look on inactive. Through you we have assigned to the demon this pot. The pot you are to deliver to the demon and send it off to the mountains of some other highland district. Should you not thus dismiss it, you shall receive a yet sterner mandate from either Sri Bhaitalu or Sri Hanuman. *" Sloka : Yaxaraxasa dustanam musha kassala bhassukaha krimi kita patangana magna sidhirvi bhishana."* *

After reading this order the *mantrician* caused seven leafen plates to be spread in as many different places, then the contents of the pot to be emptied upon them, and a black hen killed by the fellow who drove the cart. The blood he poured over the pot with the command, 'Take this pot, O demon, and begone to the mountains.' The numerous spectators who had gathered

* This *sloka* is untranslatable, and was evidently uttered *ad captandum vulgus.*

then bathed in the tank and went home. Subrahmanya, too, returned to the *choultry* with the Brahman.

After Subrahmanya returned home and related these occurrences, Rajasekhara spent some time in reflection on the superstition of the people; but that grief which flowed at the mere thought of Rukmini again burst forth, and, being unable to check it, try as he would, he finally concluded that if he went somewhere he might perhaps forget his sorrow, and accordingly set out to do the town. After walking half a dozen steps past the *choultry* he espied near a house a married couple engaged in a wordy dispute. The quarrel waxed hotter and hotter, and soon passed into a mimic war. The faster the wife heaped on the abuse, the thicker the husband showered the blows. Hearing the shouts of the man and the screams of the woman, all who lived in the street gathered in groups to see the row. But though the number thus assembled was very large, there was not found one who had come with the intention of pacifying the combatants. Everyone stood and watched the show, gaping. At this juncture Rajasekhara left the spot and moved on. In another place, a hundred yards farther on, a dozen elderly men were sitting in confab upon a street *pial*. They were evidently persons of considerable refinement, and Rajasekhara thought that he might, perhaps, drown his sorrow somewhat by noting the eloquence of their rhetoric. So he stopped short in the street and listened. Every individual in the assembly was either eulogizing his own great self, or drawing pleasure from the eulogies of his friends! Seeing them all enjoying themselves thus, and feeling downcast that there was neither any to flatter him nor to listen were he disposed to flatter, Rajasekhara concluded that it would not do for him to remain there any longer, and again moved on. He next observed four or five elegant mansions by the roadside; and conceiving the idea of entering to have a look at the interiors, he mounted the steps of one, thinking to gain admission by representing that he was a *pandit*, and had come to see the mansion.

The inhabitants of the town were, however, without exception, fond only of the rich, so his learning aided him not a whit, and as it was now nearly sundown he was forced to turn back after only an inspection of the palatial exteriors, and make his way straight to the *choultry*.

The *choultry* Brahman had no cooking to do that night, so, having a little leisure, he sat down and began to chat with Rajasekhara.

'Does your town boast of any celebrated *pandits*?' asked the latter.

'Oh yes! Harri Papayya-sastri, the court *pandit*, is here, isn't he? He won't converse with anyone at all, so he's reputed to be the greatest *pandit* of the lot. Once he came to a Brahman dinner that came off in the *choultry* here, and though he didn't talk much, he ate a heap. Even I believed him to be a great *pandit* after that.'

'Are there any others besides him?'

'Bhanumurti, our priest, is unmatched in his knowledge of theology. When I fell sick the other day he adopted an expedient fit to fetch the Millennium, and carried off ten rupees into the bargain. The day after those rascally minions of the Rajah's arrested him without cause, and put him in the lock-up, simply because some stolen goods were found in his possession.'

'Priests are for ever pointing out to their disciples the road to heaven; but as far as they themselves are concerned, they always miss the road and stumble into some pitfall even while yet in this world, and while professing such intimate knowledge of the way. It is easy enough to become a logician or a grammarian; but it is not so easy to become a *yogi*. But let that be as it may—tell us something about the condition of your townsfolk.'

'Those who labour hard find what they earn insufficient for food, clothing, and other expenses, and suffer accordingly. The lazy loons who don't work, on the other hand, enjoy the income of lands acquired by their forefathers, and dress in fine clothes and feast on half a dozen different kinds of cake and rice pudding every day. Some families who had maintained a reputation for respectability, even from the time of their great grandfathers, found it impossible to live, and long ago sought refuge under the Rajah's wing. But the Rajah's an ungracious fellow, and no matter how much they court his favour, he refuses them employment on the pretext that he can't read.'

'They never grow rich who are strangers to any higher effort than that which arises from a constant purpose to be lucky. Fortune is shy of persons who have no other business in this world than dancing attendance upon her; but befriends those who stay at home and bend their backs to the work. But what of that? Let's hear the rest of it.'

'Lots of people in the town spend their evenings in reading the *puranas*. Just a step from here there lives a person of quality. Although he never learned to read a word, he's for ever sitting with a palmleaf-book open before him. Then there's the mother of the Samaddar, who lives next door to us—she jumps for joy if you so much as mention the *puranas*. Whenever she feels the least bit sleepy, "Read me something from the *puranas*," says she. And when you begin and just get to a capital story, she stretches herself out by the wall and drops off to sleep as comfortably as you please.'

'What sort of traders have you?'

'The traders dispose of both their goods and their words at a fine profit. But no matter how much profit they make, it doesn't satisfy their greed in the least. Some of the *élite* here know this, and go at first to the shop and buy an article and give the price asked. Next they obtain some small article on credit and send around the money for it the next day. After that they gradually procure articles of greater value, and pay the prices of these also when it suits their convenience. After they've won the confidence of the shopkeepers in this way, they take a great quantity of valuable goods on pretext of a wedding or some other festivity, and finally abscond with the goods without paying an anna for them.'

'Why, if they make a business of roguery in this style, will they not lose their reputation ?'

'What does it matter about reputation ? If they only make sure of the money beforehand, with which to buy it, they can purchase as much reputation as they want afterwards.'

'I've always heard your Rajah spoken of both as a most liberal person and as one who guides his people in the path of justice. While such wicked deeds as these are going on in his very capital, does the Rajah wink at them and do nothing ?'

'What do irregularities such as these amount to ? They're not a mustard-seed's part of a pumpkin as compared with the wickedness that ran riot formerly in the time of our Maharajah's father. Why, had you come to the town at that time, do you suppose you could have walked fearlessly about the streets in broad daylight with good clothes on, as you do now ? Why, it's only because our Rajah has a thousand eyes, and is constantly punishing hosts of evil-doers, that we have now no murders and such like desperate deeds.'

'Are the religious rites prescribed by the rubric carefully observed in the town ?'

'They are performed according to rule morning, noon, and night.'

'If that's the case, have you already repeated your orisons ?'

'What, you don't suppose, do you, that I could remember until now the prayer I learned on my installation-day without forgetting it ?'

'Well, never mind that. Have you offered your libation ?'

'Yes, I have; not only the libation, but the whole of the prayer as well.'

By the time this conversation was ended the sun had

set, and Rajasekhara arose and went to dinner. After the meal he lay down and fell into a train of reflection which resulted in a determination to leave such a home for all knavery as that town, as quickly as possible. Accordingly, early the following morning he obtained a bandy, and setting out in it with his family, reached Bhimavaram by the time the sun was three hours high. The inhabitants of the place, hearing that some strangers had arrived in a cart, turned out in great force to have a look at them, and kept up a constant fire of interrogatories as to their place of abode and the cause of their coming. Both Rajasekhara and Manikyamba at length grew weary of repeating again and again to every one who asked, the answers they had already so often given. The townsfolk made this their special business, and were ready enough to come and ask questions; but no sooner did Rajasekhara hint that they were in need of a lodging than the bystanders replied that none was obtainable, and drew back as though they did not hear what he said. Rajasekhara then stopped the cart in the street and set out to look for a lodging. He was until midday going from house to house, but not a person was there in the town who would give them so much as a place in which to cook and eat their morning meal. Being new comers, the family grew sick enough, while Rajasekhara was looking about for a lodging, of gazing at the heaps of garbage piled in the streets, for they were all ignorant of the fact that this was none other than the villagers' gold—they making a business of carting it to the out-villages and selling it for manure.

Rajasekhara held his nose against the vile stench and walked on to the house of the village *karanam*. Having ascertained this person's family name, he raked up some distant relationship, and pressed the worthy disciple of the pen so hard that he finally allowed them to cook their morning meal in his house, and, moreover, called a clerical Brahman, who was a neighbour of his, and requested him to give Rajasekhara his old house in which to reside. He replied that the house could not be used as a dwelling until repaired; that it was impossible for him to give it without his wife's consent; and raised a score of other objections. Rajasekhara, however, induced him to sit down, and, after lecturing him for fully an hour on kindness to one's neighbour, slipped a couple of rupees into his hand and agreed to repair the house. More potent than the whole compendium of moral truths Rajasekhara had uttered was the money he placed in his hand. It won the Brahman's consent in a trice; so Rajasekhara at once had the cart brought around, and after they had cooked and eaten a meal at the *karanam's*, entered the house of the village priest with his family just as the lamps were being lighted. This house had been erected on marshy ground. It was wholly destitute of windows, while the walls, built in accordance with the architectural *sastra* so that the master could touch the cross-beams with his hand, were very low. The doorways, in consequence, were lower still. The result was that even they who had never stooped before walked in a stooping attitude when in this house. Sadly deficient in height though the inner walls were, the outer ones that surrounded the yard had, at all events, been built at such an elevation—perhaps from fear of burglars—that it was absolutely impossible for a breath of air to enter. When the occupants left the house, however, there being no one to take care of it, the place had gone to ruins, and was now little more than a mass of dilapidated walls through which the air found ample opportunity of effecting an entrance. When the house was occupied before, some one was constantly down sick in it; for this reason and for the further one that the daughter of the master of the house had died there, the inmates had come to the conclusion that the dwelling was occupied by an evil spirit, and hence unfit for occupation. They therefore abandoned this and moved to another place. The star under which his daughter had died was one of the five in the Archer; so the Brahman laid the house in ruins for six months, when, being still unwilling to return to it with his children, he built another, and was now living therein. After taking possession of the house, Rajasekhara provided for effective ventilation by constructing windows, had the house raised so as to get rid of the damp, and built a separate kitchen in the garden at a distance from the house. For these repairs, food, etc., the hundred rupees he had brought fast melted away, and it seemed that in two or three months at most they would be reduced to the verge of want.

Being a country place, neither milk, buttermilk, nor fuel could be bought in Bhimavaram. By giving the hulls and bran from their paddy to those who kept cows, they got a modicum of thin buttermilk. Every Sunday Rajasekhara went to Peddapuram and bought in the fair and carried home whatever supplies were needed for the week. By the time he had been a month in the place quite a number of the inhabitants struck up an acquaintance with him. When they learned his circumstances they sympathised deeply in his distress, and counselled him to see Sobhanadri-rajah, who was a relative of the Rajah, and keeper of the prison. In the near vicinity of Bhimavaram there stood at that time a fort called Syamalkota. It contained the Temple of Syamalamba; hence its name. It was at that time used as a prison, in which were kept all persons convicted of crime in the dominions of the Peddapuram Rajah. The fort is now in ruins; but a village has been built on its site which bears the name of Samalkot. Sobhanadri-rajah, the commander of the fort, was also the proprietor of the village.

During the time Rajasekhara resided in the place Ramarajah was in the habit of occasionally coming to see them by night.

Made anxious by the gradual melting away of their means, Manikyamba daily urged her husband to see Sobhanadri-rajah and make an effort to secure a position. Two or three times he went, and as often returned with the excuse that no opportunity had presented itself of seeing the Rajah. The last time Rajasekhara attempted to obtain audience of Sobhanadri-rajah the following conversation transpired between him and his worthy spouse:

'Did you get audience of the Rajah?' queried Manikyamba.

'I did. While standing in the street door I caught sight of a servant and asked if I might go inside. He replied that if I was rich I might go straight in; but if poor, there I must remain. After reflecting a few moments I made bold to enter, and soon stood before the Rajah.'

'Did you address him, and acquaint him with your affairs in a becoming manner?'

'I went into the room and made known my circumstances without reserve. Perhaps you ask, "Who with?" Not with the Rajah; for, long as I talked, not a word escaped from the Rajah's mouth. No sooner did I begin to talk than a dog near the bed began to bark. So I suppose I talked with it. But what it said I failed to grasp, since I'm not versed in dog lore. While I was standing there in doubt as to what it meant, the Rajah called a servant and commanded in a language I knew, to "Send this Brahman out." Twigging what was about to happen, I retreated quietly on my own account before he came up, and came straight home.'

Having no particular inclination further to court the favour of a Rajah who had treated him with such marked respect, and cogitating as to how they were to get a living in the future, Rajasekhara concluded that he must send Subrahmanya off somewhere. He mentioned the matter to Manikyamba, and, with her consent, spoke to his son about it. He agreed to the proposal with great joy; so they set their wits to work and finally concluded to send him to Pitapuram. On the day fixed for the journey Rajasekhara called his son to him, and after giving him many injunctions, intermixed with much good advice, and charging him again and again to walk in the path of uprightness, he blessed the kneeling lad and furnished him with five rupees for expense.

Manikyamba, too, without perceptibly diminishing the stock she had in hand, showered upon him all the blessings the occasion demanded. Poor Subrahmanya, weeping that the time had now come for him to leave them, kissed his little sister—slipping one of the rupees his father had given him into her hand as he did so—took leave of them all, and trudged off with many lingering looks behind.

CHAPTER X.

Friendship with Sobhanadri-rajah—Preparations for Sita's Wedding—News of Ranamurti's Death—Difference with Ramarajah—Rajasekhara is Thrown into Prison—The Abduction of Sita.

ABOUT eight o'clock one Sunday morning Rajasekhara was on his way to Peddapuram, when Sobhanadri-rajah, who was sitting upon an elevated seat in the street *pial*, caught sight of him, and directed his servant to 'go and fetch the Brahman who was passing along the road.' This person at once came running up at the top of his speed and informed Rajasekhara that 'the Rajah had given permission for him to approach.' Rajasekhara's one great desire was to ingratiate himself with the Rajah at any cost; so without waiting for a second invitation he crossed over and took his seat upon the bench which the Rajah pointed out to him.

'You're the person, are you not,' asked Sobhanadri-rajah, 'who came from Bhimavaram lately, and is now living in Somabhatlu's house ?'

'I am. I visited you once before.'

'We remember. We were then engaged in the transaction of very important business and became angry with you. Besides, we did not know at the time that you were the newcomer. What number of a family have you dependent upon you for a living? It's reported, too, I think, that you have a marriageable daughter ?'

'I have at present but one daughter eligible for mar-

riage. My eldest daughter died on the road when we
were attacked by the robbers. I sent my son to Pitapuram just after coming here, to find employment of
some sort.'

While this conversation was in progress a number of
the leading men of the place dropped in and seated
themselves on the bench in the *pial*. To these the
Rajah bragged incessantly of his wonderful exploits;
and as his utterances were wholly devoid of wit, his
auditors supplied the deficiency with excessive laughter.
Thinking it might give offence if he alone remained
quiet when the whole company was roaring, Rajasekhara,
too, though seeing nothing worth even so much as a
smile, got into the habit of pretending to laugh whenever the rest did. At first the Rajah touched lightly on
the various topics introduced, in such a way as to lead
Rajasekhara to think him a well-informed man; but he
soon began to conduct himself as though he knew everything. When he could think of nothing more to say,
he would gaze into the faces of those present and laugh
vacantly. This led the assembly to incessantly eulogize
his learning. Had not some musicians come up in the
meantime and begun to sing a song, it is safe to say that
their flatteries would not have ceased until the gathering
dispersed. As soon as the musicians began to sing, the
thoughts of all turned towards home; but, fearful of the
Rajah's displeasure should they leave so abruptly, they
managed, not without much difficulty and muttering to
themselves, to keep their seats for a little longer. At
last one of the principal auditors, unable longer to endure
the interminable song, broke in with 'It's not right for
these people to trouble his honour as though eulogizing
him were their special business. So you may now order
them to stop singing.' The company unanimously pronounced this the proper thing, and at once the gathering
broke up. While the company were dispersing the
Rajah asked Rajasekhara if he would not come occasionally and visit him. He replied that he would be
delighted to do so; and, as it was then near midday,

abandoned his trip to Peddapuram for the time and returned home.

From that time forward Rajasekhara paid daily visits to Sobhanadri-rajah both morning and evening. The Rajah invariably received him with marked favour, and put him at ease with suave words. Even when he was engaged in the transaction of state business, Rajasekhara stood near and looked on. When the clerks read petitions written by the residents of the surrounding villages, he observed that while the real petition was crowded into the last two or three lines, the title alone completely filled the first two pages; and he began to derive great pleasure from the thought that his honour the Rajah boasted far more honorary titles than the residents of these villages. State business over, the Rajah would begin to chat with the company. It mattered not to what length he spun it out, his own prowess formed the one theme of his discourse. Although these same yarns had been listened to a dozen times before, the whole company would laugh each time they were repeated, precisely as they had laughed the first time. Some would gratify the Rajah's vanity by reciting eulogistic verses which they had prepared. It seemed hardly right to Rajasekhara to be the only one silent where all were so loud in their eulogiums. Since, however, he was without experience in the art of flattery, and was, moreover, fearful of uttering what was untrue, he praised the Rajah for the fine clothes he wore, since he was worthy of praise in no other particular. Even though he failed to gain anything else by thus conducting himself at court, he at least learned the secret of raising a general laugh in company, for he soon acquired the habit of laughing first of all at his own utterances, seeing which the others would laugh too. Occasionally the Rajah would deliver a lecture on virtue. No matter how hard one toiled in this world, he said, 'twas simply for his food; and so, do what one would in that respect, 'twas no harm. It was owing to this maxim being so deeply rooted in his own mind, perhaps, that the Rajah spent his time daily from the moment he awoke until eleven o'clock solely in making provision for his breakfast; from breakfast-time his one anxiety was whether he should succeed in getting any lunch; while no sooner was lunch over than he began to consider what relishes there were for dinner.

By these constant comings and goings, Rajasekhara became exceedingly intimate with the Rajah. Learning this, the Brahmans would go to his house and chat over various matters, and some of them ask, in the course of conversation, whether he had thought of giving Sita to anyone in marriage. To this he would reply, that having no money on hand at present, he hadn't bothered his head about betrothing her. One day while Rajasekhara was taking his ease after his meal, Bommaganti Subbarayadu the astrologer came in, and began vaunting his endless learning in astrology, and the celebrity he had attained thereby. He stated that all the *élite* of the Telugu country sent their horoscopes to him to ascertain the issues, and in proof of this, produced a pile of calculations of nativities, purporting to have been written for the Rajahs of Vizianagram and other distant territories. He then asked Rajasekhara to fetch the record of his nativity in order that he might tell him its issue.

'My confidence in astrology is all gone,' replied Rajasekhara; 'not a single forecast of all the horoscopes our people had written, and for which my wealth was plundered from me ever came true. When we set out on the Benares pilgrimage, we left home at what had been fixed upon as a lucky time, yet we encountered great dangers on the way. Through that I lost my faith in astrology. And so for the same reason, when I came here from Peddapuram the other day, I started without fixing any time whatever.'

But mine is no common astrology. No divination of mine or time that I fixed ever yet missed. Whatever number of symbols I write in a nativity, just so many symbols must come true.'

'Even though the result be as you say, I want nothing to do with it. Should you declare beforehand that the result will be good, 'twould be very disheartening if what I had anticipated failed to come; while should it really come, I could not obtain any very great amount of pleasure from it because of having anticipated it so long. If you declare that evil will result, I shall not only be under the necessity of grieving when it comes, but shall be a prey to anxiety from this very moment. If, on the other hand, it shouldn't come at all, then I'll have had all this fool's sorrow for nothing. From such needless anxiety evil is sure to spring, while from rejoicing good alone can never come.'

'It is very unbecoming for you, a *pandit*, to go on in this style. We must never lose our confidence in *sastras* written by the ancients. But let that go. It seems that your daughter has reached marriageable age. Why do you longer neglect making some attempt to get her married?'

'I am myself cogitating on that very matter. I've seen no suitable match—besides that, I see no money in hand. There isn't a good alliance anywhere to your knowledge, is there?'

'Al-li-ance? There is—but—they're great folk. It's doubtful whether they'd marry into your family. If you could manage it, 'twould be a capital union for you in every respect.'

'Where do they reside? and what must we do to bring about the match?'

'Their place of residence is Peddapuram. Their family name is Manchirajah. They have lands that yield them an annual income of two thousand rupees, and they're reported to have plenty of cash besides. The young fellow is the first of the family to marry, and he's handsome. He has an elder brother, but he's also without family. This same young fellow will presently fall heir to the whole property. The bridegroom's name is Padmarajah. If we could only secure

Sobhanadri-rajah's aid, the match would certainly take place on the strength of your good luck. But in no other way is it possible.'

'If that's the case, won't you first approach the Rajah on the subject and ascertain his views?'

'I'll go ahead and find a seat. Afterwards do you come too. I'll take care in the course of our talk to bring up the subject of your daughter's marriage while you are there. At that you must join in and make known your wish to the Rajah.'

With these words astrologer Subbarayadu started off to Sobhanadri-rajah's house, where he seated himself. A few moments later Rajasekhara also came in. After conversing for a short time on various topics, the astrologer adroitly introduced the matter of Rajasekhara's daughter.

'Is your honour,' asked he, 'acquainted with the fact that Rajasekhara has a daughter desirous of marrying?'

'We are aware of the fact,' replied Sobhanadri-rajah; 'we heard but recently. Is the girl of marriageable age?'

'I saw her at noon this very day. It won't do to keep her any longer. A younger girl than this one attained to puberty in my relative's village the other day.'

'Have you thought of any particular alliance?'

'There's Manchirajah Padmarajah in Peddapuram. If you would but help, a match might be arranged there.'

'True, it's a capital connection. But would he be willing to marry this girl?'

'It will never do,' broke in Rajasekhara, 'for your honour to fail to make some effort to secure us this favour. Once you have made known your wishes, they won't act in opposition to them.'

'Padmarajah came in this morning,' replied Sobhanadri-rajah. 'We'll speak to him about it while you are here. Ho! Swamiga! Manchirajah Padmarajah is probably talking with our brother-in-law. Go and tell him we said he was to look in for a moment before he leaves—without fail.'

A short time after the departure of the servant, there walked in a dark man of thirty years of age, wearing white bleached clothes, rings on his ten fingers, bracelets on his arms, and a gold necklace on his neck. Sobhanadri-rajah politely invited him to be seated, and motioned him to a place at his side.

'Swamigardu,' remarked the newcomer, 'informed me that your honour wanted me, and so I returned at once, although already on my way. Have you anything that you wish to communicate to me?'

'This gentleman,' replied Sobhanadri-rajah, 'has been living in our village for some time. He is a very respectable man. His name is Rajasekhara. He has heard that you are thinking of marriage. He has a daughter—why shouldn't you marry her? The girl is very beautiful; while their family is good, and has long been a right orthodox one.'

'There are a lot of people about who say they'll give their girls. Hitherto I've had no desire whatever to enter into matrimony. Had I had, I'd have been married in my early youth and been blessed with a family by this time. But when people in your position wring one's neck, one must consent whether or no. However, I'll inform my elder brother what your honour's wish is in regard to the matter, and let you know to-morrow whatever his decision may be.'

'Be sure and tell your brother that we directed you to say that, in case he should not listen to us now, this is the conclusion of our friendship with him.'

'Very good. He'll not act contrary to your command. I shall take leave.'

After Padmarajah had taken his departure, Rajasekhara implored Sobhanadri-rajah again and again to make a special effort to compass so desirable an alliance. The Rajah gave his word that he would do everything in his power to bring about the match, and confidently asserted that, could the union but be accomplished, Rajasekhara would enjoy greater respectability and renown than ever before. As it was now sunset the Rajah rose for dinner, and the remaining company made their salaams and departed to their homes.

The sun was but two hours high on the following day when Rajasekhara came in; but Sobhanadri-rajah immediately left his room to receive him.

'Do you know,' said he smiling gleefully, 'the answer to the message we sent yesterday actually came last night?'

'What was the answer? What was the answer?' eagerly asked Rajasekhara.

'After I had sent so pressing an invitation, do you think they would decline it? They wrote a note saying they'd marry her,' replied he, putting a palm-leaf roll into Rajasekhara's hand.

Rajasekhara received it with every manifestation of delight; and the Rajah sent him at once to call astrologer Subbarayadu to determine a suitable time for the wedding. After referring to the *panchanga* and reflecting for a moment, the savant fixed the time in the sign Aries and constellation Punarvassu, at six and one half minutes after twelve o'clock on the night of Thursday the seventh of the wane of the month Vaisakha. Sobhanadri-rajah observed that it would be necessary to commence the preparations for the wedding immediately; and, adding that if Rajasekhara was in want of money, he might take this amount for the present and repay it when convenient, opened his box and handed him one hundred rupees. He then called a servant and placed him at Rajasekhara's disposal, with directions to remain in attendance for a week, and to do whatever he was told. Accepting this assistance gladly, Rajasekhara returned home.

From that day forward Rajasekhara was constantly trotting back and forth to Peddapuram, buying *dhal* and other articles of the kind, and fetching pot-herbs from the Sunday fair. They finished all preparations for the wedding, and got Sita ready* for that event on the fifth. When it wanted yet a night of the time fixed for the wedding ceremony, that is, on the night of the sixth, just at dark there came a cooly carrying a stick in his hand, and closely wrapped in a blanket, who handed Sita a palm-leaf roll—he had brought a letter, he said, from Rajahmundry. Manikyamba came out just then and took the letter from Sita's hand. Rajasekhara had gone to Peddapuram and hadn't yet returned; but as it was now past the usual time of his arrival, the cooly was to wait in the street until he came, she said, and disappeared in the house. As Rajasekhara was rather late that evening the cooly grew impatient; so Manikyamba gave him a pint of rice and some coppers and sent him off. A moment later Sita went to the door to see whether her father was coming, and found there a staff, which they, supposing the cooly who had just gone to have dropped, placed in a corner of the bedroom to be returned to him should he come back for it.

In a little while Rajasekhara arrived. As soon as his wife told him a letter had come from Rajahmundry, and gave it into his hand, he took it to the light; but he had not read it half through when the letter fell from his trembling hands to the floor and tears began to stream from his eyes. Manikyamba was standing by to hear what the epistle contained. Alarmed at her husband's gestures, and unable to account for his sudden grief, she begged him to tell her what the trouble was. In choked accents he replied that their relative, Ramamurti, had breathed his last at noon the day previous, of cholera; and over this sad intelligence they grieved long in concert.

Early on the morning of the next day, Rajasekhara proceeded to Sobhanadri-rajah's house, and informed him of the misfortune which had befallen them in the death of his cousin Ramamurti; and, after expressing

---

* Literally, 'Made her bride'—*i.e.*, by bathing and anointing. A similar ceremony is performed on the same day by the parents of the bridegroom.

his sorrow at the loss and delay to the wedding which must inevitably occur through the time for that event falling just when they were in defilement for the dead, he begged that a messenger might be sent to the bridegroom's people immediately so as to prevent their starting. Sobhanadri-rajah consoled him as far as it lay in his power, and at once despatched a messenger to Peddapuram. Rajasekhara then returned home.

On the following Sunday Rajasekhara, after his morning meal, transported to Peddapuram by means of coolies a number of *kavadies* of vegetables for the purpose of disposing of them in the fair. While standing about after selling his produce to a shopkeeper at a bargain, an adult, wearing a turban and a long coat, approached and accosted him with—

'Hallo, brother! what defilement have you suffered that you wear that *bottu?*'

Rajasekhara stood stupefied and unable to command a word, gazing into the speaker's face. Again the respectable-looking party demanded:

'You've got on a sandal-wood patch—what defilement are we under?'

The speaker was no other than Ramamurti himself!

'You remember, don't you, my sending you the news of our Rukmini's death?' replied Rajasekhara after his first transport of joy at again seeing his cousin alive; 'well, we had arranged Sita's wedding for the day before yesterday, Thursday, and were all ready for the event, when on Wednesday evening along came some base wretch when I was out, and handed your sister-in-law a letter stating that you were dead.'

'Someone has adopted this wicked device for the purpose of frustrating the marriage.'

'He was no well-wisher who planned the affair. But come along home with me and see your sister-in-law and Sita.'

'I've just now got to see the Rajah, and return to Rajahmundry without delay on state business. But in a month's time I'll come over again and spend a couple of days with you,' replied Ramamurti as he turned away towards the Rajah's court for the purpose of transacting his business.

Rajasekhara went straight to Bhimavaram and told his wife the good news about Ramamurti, cursing copiously the villain who had balked the marriage. At that moment Sita brought the staff which the cooly had dropped on his departure, and showed it to her father. No sooner had he taken it in his hand and examined it than he recognised it as Ramarajah's. It was, he declared to his wife, the very one he had shown him but a short time before. On further reflection, they both concluded for a certainty that the fellow who brought the letter could have been none other than Ramarajah.

'But why,' mused Rajasekhara, 'why should Ramajah, who of all people is under obligation to us, do such a thing?'

''Twas only the other night;' added Manikyamba, 'that he saved our lives and showed us so much kindness. I can guess no reason whatever why he should meditate such a piece of villany as this.'

'He may have taken money from our enemies and brought himself to commit this evil deed,' suggested her husband; 'money makes enemies of even the dearest friends, you know.'

'Greed of gain in his present circumstances may have led him to commit this folly. But see! There comes Ramarajah himself! If you ask him about it, all will be plain.'

'What, Sir! Ramarajah!' called out Rajasekhara; 'considering that we did you so great a kindness, is it charitable in you to balk our plans in this way?'

'How have I balked your plans?'

'Didn't you trump up a letter to the effect that our Ramamurti was dead, and give it to my people when I was out?'

'I haven't so much as seen the inside of your house while you were out. And I want you to understand that if you impute such base actions to me, you and I'll not get along together.'

'If you haven't so much as seen the inside of my house, how did this stick of yours come here?'

'I've been unable to find my stick for five or six days back, and have been looking everywhere for it. Ah, now I see! You carried off the stick yourself, and now you're laying the blame on me, so's to escape. I always supposed you to be some sort of honest people.'

'And pray what dishonesty have you spied out in me? Do you* never again cross the threshold of my house!'

'Don't you *nivu* me. Who wants anything to do with your house?' demanded Ramarajah, starting up and leaving them abruptly.

Immediately after Rajasekhara, too, went out. Proceeding to the house of Sobhanadri-rajah he related to him all that had occurred, and begged him to call the astrologer for the purpose of again fixing a time for the wedding.

'The night of the very day on which he fixed the time before in your house,' replied Sobhanadri-rajah, 'the astrologer took the fever. The disease grew so bad that he lost all desire to live; so at noon on Tuesday they laid him on the ground.† Thereupon all his relatives came together, and thinking such a death an improper one for an educated Brahman to die, administered extreme unction. From that very night the disease turned, and they say he is now quite convalescent. Do you go at once and return here after, ascertaining at what time this month the marriage should come off.'

'Very good. I shall take leave;' and Rajasekhara, suiting the action to the word, rose and proceeded without delay to the house of astrologer Subbarayadu. Finding the astrologer seated on a bench in the porch,

---

* *Nivu*, the second person singular, used only in addressing inferiors.

† See also the account of the death of Subbamma, p. 82. Brahmins invariably deposit the dying upon the ground.

leaning against the wall, he saluted him and hoped he was much better.

'I am somewhat better,' replied the astrologer; 'when my complaint was at its worst and I was unconscious, all my kinsfolk gathered with the intention of making away with my goods, and administered absolution to me. It is but six months since my wife by my second marriage came to live with me. I haven't enjoyed a single year's unbroken happiness with her yet, and as soon as I get stronger they won't so much as allow me to stay in the house, but will hunt me out of it.'

'What's the use of crying over spilt milk? Banish all thought of domestic felicity from your mind, and pass your remaining time in reflecting upon your approaching dissolution, and in what is more essential in your present state—the repetition of the *pranava*.'*

'I have already severed all earthly ties. You must forget and forgive the injury I did you.'

'Why, what injury have you ever done me?'

'The ancients say that if past sin be confessed, 'twill be remitted. The fellow to whom you gave Sita in marriage the other day is not a rich man. He's a pimp who procures harlots for Sobhanadri-rajah. The clothes, bracelets, and all the other things he wore, are the Rajah's. The Rajah planned the whole affair and sent me to you. I carried out the scheme. It had already been thus foreordained of God, and so the affair passed off successfully. So, as you just said, what's the use of crying over spilt milk?'

'Is Sobhanadri-rajah such a base wretch? When I first went to visit him, I guessed what manner of man he was. But when he put the rupees into my hand, I, ignorant of this base deception, supposed he gave them simply out of regard for me. Had the wedding not fallen through by Ramarajah's charity, it would have been an accomplished fact. Had it not been for him,

---

* The mystic syllable OM, the repetition of which is believed to ensure salvation.

we would certainly have cut the child's throat without cause.'

'The marriage not taken place? I hear good news! How did what was as good as done fall through?'

'News of our defilement by the death of a relative reached us; so the happy event did not come off at the time you fixed. That villain just now sent me to call you for the very purpose of fixing the time anew.'

'Don't talk to me any longer about that evil doer. The very day I fixed the date for the wedding in your house at that sinner's direction, this complaint set in; so, believing that God had brought this affliction upon me as a punishment for the deceit I'd practised upon you, I vowed by ten million gods to make a clean breast of the whole truth, and obtain absolution from my sin, should I recover before the marriage was consummated. But I didn't recover in time. Then I called to mind the maxim of Sukra:

> 'Of maidens fair and marriage matters grave,
> Of life or wealth or woman's virtue ta'en—
> A herd of cows or Brahmin's life to save—
> Thou mayest lie, O Rajah, without bane,'

and pacified my conscience somewhat by the reflection that I had only lied about a marriage. Probably it was on the strength of the same maxim that no one else said anything to you about Padmarajah.'

'I'll go at once and ask Sobhanadri-rajah about the affair, and say to his very face whatever needs to be said.'

Suiting the action to the word Rajasekhara started off, and found Sobhanadri-rajah standing in his street-door. 'I believed your words,' cried Rajasekhara 'to be those of a man of some honour; but in that I was deceived. Is it because I have been on friendly terms with you so long, that you attempt to marry my daughter to a worthless wretch?'

With these words he was turning away when Sobhanadri-rajah called out, 'Return the rupees you got from us, and then be off about your business.'

'I spent the rupees you gave me, and my own as well in the purchase of articles for the wedding. I have now no money. When I have it in hand I'll repay you,' replied Rajasekhara again turning away.

Sobhanadri-rajah at once directed his servants to seize him and cast him into prison.

From the moment Manikyamba heard this news she fell to brooding over the calamity which had befallen her husband, renounced food and sleep, and spent her whole time in religious meditations, interrupted at intervals by pining grief.

Three days after this occurrence, Sita was standing in the street door just at dawn when two strangers accosted her, stating that her brother had come from Pitapuram and was then in the house of the *laranam* in the next street, whence he had sent them to fetch her. On this pretence they took Sita to the outskirts of the village, when they lifted her between them and ran off at the top of their speed. Manikyamba no sooner heard this piece of bad news than she fell to the ground in a swoon. After regaining consciousness she would listen to no consolations, but bewailed incessantly with copious floods of tears the hard separation from her husband and her daughter's sad fate.

CHAPTER XI.

Subrahmanya reaches Pitapuram—A Friend meets him and makes him Welcome to his Home—Narrative of Niladri-rajah—The Rajah's Money disappears—They use the Magic Eyesalve—The Lost Treasure is found in Niladri-rajah's Yard with a Quantity of other Valuables.

THE day he left his parents, Subrahmanya lost his way, and after wandering he knew not where, finally reached Pitapuram just at dusk. It happened that at that moment a number of evil-minded persons, who were seated in a certain place, caught sight of him, and observing his forlorn condition, and concluding from his manner that he was a rustic, determined to bully the lad and get what they could out of him. One of the group at once started up, and, advancing into the road by which Subrahmanya was approaching, blocked his advance, and demanded, 'Who comes there?'

'I'm a Brahman,' replied Subrahmanya; 'I'm coming from Bhimarvaram.'

'What's the reason you enter the place when it is so dark?'

'Had I walked straight on from the time I started, I'd have got here while it was yet daylight; but I missed the way and took the wrong road, and so I'm late, as you see.'

'Have you any relatives in the place?'

'I have no relatives here. I've come to wait on the Rajah and obtain work.'

'Whose is that bundle on your shoulder?'

'Mine, of course. What would I be doing with another person's bundle?'

'It is not yours. You seem a suspicious character. I shan't let you off yet awhile. Along with you to the station.'

'I'm no thief. I've been most respectable from my very childhood. Let me go.'

'The Rajah's order is not to let anyone off who enters the town after dark. But what will you give me if I let you go?'

'I'll give you four annas. Let me go.'

'It can't be done under four rupees. You look like the very rascal I'm after. Put the bundle down. If you don't do as I tell you, look out, or you'll get something for yourself.'

Just then a man who had shortly before gone to the outskirts of the village and was now returning, happened along that very road on his way home, and hearing the row, stopped and asked, 'What are you annoying that man for?'

'See here,' cried Subrahmanya, 'this fellow says that he won't let me go unless I give him four rupees. He's restraining me by force.'

'What, Subrahmanya! is it you?' cried the stranger. 'I recognized your voice at once. What are you doing here alone at this time of night? You haven't run away from home secretly, have you? But come, let us go to the house.'

'Why, Umapati, how did you come here? Had you been a moment later, it's hard to say what that fellow would have done to me.'

'What fellow? Where's the person who was bothering you?'

'Seeing us talking he slipped off, and—there he is, running away yonder in the distance.'

'Let him go. We'll see what can be done about him to-morrow.'

Conversing with each other thus, the pair in company walked towards the house, and by the time they had arrived there Subrahmanya had related to his companion the misfortunes which, up to that time, had befallen his father and family, their then circumstances, and the reason of his coming to Pitapuram. Umapati, while deeply grieved at this sad intelligence, expressed his astonishment that the abundant wealth which Rajasekhara enjoyed when he studied with him had melted away so entirely, and left its whilom possessor in so poverty-stricken a condition; and he determined to spare no effort on behalf of the priest who had educated him, but to do him every kindness that lay in his power. He therefore gave Subrahmanya a most hearty welcome, informed him that he was in the enjoyment of a position, under the Pitapuram Rajah, worth twenty rupees a month, and told him that he would endeavour to induce the Rajah to provide him with a situation equally good. Subrahmanya was, he added, to regard his house as his home until he obtained this employment. Accordingly, every day after their meal, Subrahmanya accompanied Umapati to the Rajah's court. His Highness, Vijayarama, Maharajah of Pitapuram, one day observed the strange lad, and asked Umapati who he was. Whereupon Umapati narrated the story of his friend's family from beginning to end, and ended by preferring a request that His Highness might be pleased to grant him some post at court.

On the road which ran from Umapati's house to the fort, stood a spacious mansion. A rajah had rented this building, and occupied it with his suite for a month past. A few days before he had honoured the Brahmans of the place with a dinner. It comes naturally to everybody to eat to repletion when they get it for nothing; and these worthy Brahmans, though accustomed to season their food with but a few drops of *ghi* when at home, for once in their lives, at least, drank this oleaginous delicacy by the quart. This dinner made the rajah famous throughout the town; so much so, that crowds came daily to court his favour. His name was Niladri-rajah. One day as Niladri-rajah was taking his morning constitutional on the street *pial* after breakfast, he caught sight of Subrahmanya passing at a distance, and signalled that he wished to speak with him.

'It seems to us,' said he, 'that we've seen you somewhere before. To what place do you belong?'

'My native place is Dhavalesvaram. Our family name is Khotêti. My name is Subrahmanya.'

'Ah, we recollect! Aren't you Rajasekhara's son? Where is he at present?'

'He's in Bhimavaram. Where did you know him?'

'It was in Dhavalesvaram that we saw him. A year ago, while on a pilgrimage, we spent ten days in Dhavalesvaram. While there we bathed in the Godaveri, visited Kotiphali and other celebrated shrines, and came here a month ago to visit the shrine of Pādagāya. Here we've been ever since. Your worthy father regarded us as his priest. While we were there your good father was never away from our side.'

'I have no recollection of seeing you a year ago. Where did you lodge?'

'You don't recollect, but we do very well. Let me see—you should have a couple of sisters. Are they well?'

'My elder sister, Rukmini, is dead. The younger one is well.'

'You're not very well acquainted with our affairs, I fancy. The Vizianagram Rajah is our maternal uncle's son. She that was married to the Rajah of Mogaliturra is our cousin by our father's joint wife.'

'Just now I'm on my way to court. I'll call some other time when I have leisure, and have a talk. Will you grant me leave for the present?' said Subrahmanya, rising; and having made his devoir, he proceeded on his way to the Rajah's hall of audience. This was now an everyday business with him; for he never flagged in his attendance at court, where he struck up an acquaintance with all the officials, and acquired much valuable information about the details of State business. Whenever the clerks had a document to write, they would, without exception, call Subrahmanya, and have him draw it up for them. Whenever an account was to be squared, they would have no one to do it but Subrahmanya. For this he got not an anna of pay; but, so far as work went, his position was superior to that of the salaried clerks. No matter what or how much work they asked him to do, he was always ready to go at it. By this means he soon won the goodwill of the whole office; and one day the clerks went in a body and represented to the Rajah that this lad had long been serving and expecting a situation, and begged His Highness to grant him one. To this the Rajah replied that when an opening presented itself, he would confer the post upon him; in the meantime he was to remain in attendance at the palace.

Meanwhile Subrahmanya had one day again called on Niladri-rajah, who greeted him cordially.

'Well, Master Subrahmanya, what's the news in town?'

'Nothing of moment. I'm still waiting the Rajah's pleasure for a situation. I haven't got into work yet.'

'Why should you wait so long? Can you undertake a journey to a foreign country? We'll get you a capital situation, without the slightest difficulty, under the Maharajah of Vizianagram. He's our mother's younger sister's son.'

This last assertion not agreeing with his former statement that this Rajah was the son of his maternal uncle, Subrahmanya inferred that he was lying; but his proposal was so magnanimous that the lad was pleased, and made no reply.

'Well,' demanded Niladri-rajah, 'what are you hesitating about? As sure as you're alive we'll get you a capital situation. Why, the strongest friendship exists between Ramavarma, the Rajah of Kalahasti, and ourselves. When we were little, he and we rode in the same carriage together. This is a great secret—you're not to tell anyone.'

'All right. If I don't get into work here, I'll certainly come.'

'We'll tell you another secret. In our youth, we and the Kalahasti Rajah used to gamble together. His affairs are nothing to us, of course; but, you see, he kept a dancing-girl at that time.'

'Your honour is wearing the rice *bottu* very early in the morning. Do you perform the *pardhiva*?' *

'I used to do the *pardhiva*; but at present I perform *Siva pujah*. Report says, I think, that your Rajah is also very much devoted to the *Siva pujah*. It is by this means, so we've heard, that he became so rich.'

'Yes, I too have heard that he's very wealthy.'

'How much money is your Rajah reported to have by him?'

'The common report is that it's not less than ten *lacs*.'

'The whole of it is kept in the fort, I suppose?'

'The whole of it is kept in the fort. A corps of old veterans, who have long served faithfully, is on guard there.'

* *Pardhiva*, the worship of an earthen *linga*, performed at early morning. *Siva pujah*, worship of the stone *linga*, performed usually at mid-day.

'The Maharajah of Vizianagram thinks of erecting a new fort, and charged us expressly to procure plans of the forts in all the towns we visited. Only the other day we secured a plan of the Peddapuram fort. Couldn't you draw a diagram of this one too, and let us have it?'

'Certainly. Fetch paper and pen; I'll strike it off and give it you at once,' replied Subrahmanya.

When paper and pens had been brought in, he drew from memory a plan of all he had seen in the fort, and handed it to Niladrirajah. That worthy took the paper, and began at once to ask questions about the uses to which the various sections were put, and about the solidity of the wall. To these Subrahmanya went on to give suitable replies so far as he knew the particulars.

'It's on the north side, next the street, is it not—the treasury?' asked Niladri-rajah.

'Yes.'

'It's all first-rate; but how high did they build the walls?'

'It's probably about twelve feet.'

'You must keep the matter dark, and tell no one about our having drawn a plan of the fort. Rajahs don't like the idea of there being another fort similar to their own.'

With this parting caution Niladri-rajah called for betel and leaf, which he presented to Subrahmanya, and dismissed him with the assurance that when the fort was erected he would not fail to inform his Highness that he was the person who had drawn the plan. Pleased with this promise, Subrahmanya took his departure and wended his way slowly homeward, building all sorts of castles in the air on the strength of the hope that he might, perhaps, obtain a position of emolument.

Early one morning, several days after the events just narrated, a rumour became current in the town that thieves had broken into the Rajah's palace and carried off the jewels and money from the treasury. A little later the Rajah's servants began to raise the hue and cry, and to visit all parts of the town, seizing all who were unfriendly to them, and dragging them off to the station, where those in charge locked them up in the cells and proceeded to torture them in various ways to compel them to confess the crime. Large numbers of innocent persons were thus seized and tortured; but the police were wholly unable to get any clue to the real thieves. On the north side of the fort there were footprints as though the burglars had reared a ladder against the wall and thus effected an entrance. In the stone wall of the treasure-room they had pierced a hole as large as a small doorway. Had three able men undertaken to dig such an opening, it would have taken them at least half a day. There was therefore no room for conjecture as to what had become of the sleep of the thieves who had been up and hard at work so much of the night; it had, in double measure, fled for refuge to the warders. It was, however, whispered in the town that when the chink of rupees was heard in the vault, the men who stood guard supposed it to be the Goddess of Riches groaning, and rushed in terror into a strong room, where they saved their lives by barricading the door. Which of these hypotheses is correct the Allwise alone knows; but it is certain at all events that the *Diva Pecunia* left the fort that night by the new door, mounted upon human shoulders. Notwithstanding all their efforts, the royal servants could find no trace of the thieves; so at length, worn out, they went to the captain and gave a detailed report of their strenuous efforts. The captain was greatly perplexed as to what course to pursue; but after a moment's reflection he concluded to lay the blame upon some one of the royal employés; for he knew that if he failed to catch the thieves and recover the money, he would incur the Rajah's displeasure. With this object in view he examined all who frequented the court; but fearing that if he charged any of them they would be angry with him, he decided to lay the blame upon one of the subordinates. Considering it improper, however, for

himself to appear as the accuser, he proceeded to his
house, and, after talking the matter over with certain
parties, sent out for a person reported to be skilled in
the use of the magic eye-salve. In the course of three
hours he put in an appearance.

'See, here, Bhimanna,' said he as the diviner entered,
'last night some treasure was stolen from the Rajah's
palace. If you can name the man who took that money,
your fortune's made.'

'How long will that take? If you can bring back
the cash, I'll apply the collyrium and tell you the name
in a twinkling.'

'Have you got the collyrium by you now, ready
made?'

'I have. But it won't have any effect upon anyone
but a cat-eyed man.* You must have some such person
called.'

On hearing this the captain summoned a servant.

'Here, you, go and fetch Samigardu the washerman,'
said he, sending him off.

The servant started on his errand without delay, and
in the course of an hour returned, accompanied by
Samigardu. In the meantime the diviner had had a
servant-maid clean a room with cowdung, in one corner
of which he lighted a large oil-lamp. After bathing, he
entered the room and drew before the lamp a design in
flour, in which he placed an image of Anjaneya and a
casket of eye-unguent,† after which he proceeded to
make *pujah*. As soon as the washerman came in the
diviner brought his *pujah* to an end, seated the washerman in the middle of the drawing, rubbed some of the
eye-unguent from the casket in the palm of his right
hand, and bade him gaze steadily at it, and describe
everything that appeared.

'Put your hand close to the light,' said he, 'and look

---

* *I.e.*, a blue-eyed man.

† *Katuka* or *anjana*, a mixture of lampblack and oil applied by
Hindu women to the eyelids to increase the brilliancy of the eyes.
This unguent is believed to possess magic properties.

at it without winking. Is anything visible to you now ?'

'No,' replied Samigardu, 'nothing but the lampblack.'

'Don't let your sight wander. Do you see anything now ?'

'It's showing now. It looks like a big gold plate.'

'Is there anything in the centre of the plate ?'

'There's an *avisi* tree.'

'It's not an *avisi*, it's an *asoka*. See who is in the branches of the tree.'

'There's a big monkey.'

'Call him not a monkey. 'Tis the blessed Anjaneya! Make him a salutation in your mind and see what he'll say.'

'He's moving his lips over something; but I can't catch the words.'

'Ask him who made away with the Rajah's money.'

'He says without doubt 'twas one of the people who are in attendance on the Rajah.'

'Ask his family name.'

'Kōti.'

'Ask his other name, too.'

'Subbama.'

'Subrahmanya? Kōtêti Subrahmanya!'

'You didn't say it that way a little while ago,' protested the washerman.

'Is it with Anjaneya you're talking? Do you mean to say that Anjaneya didn't pronounce it so just now? That's just what he did say. 'Twas you who couldn't get the name into your mouth and pronounced it wrong. That'll do now—get up. And, look you, keep your mouth shut about this.'

With this admonition he pushed Samigardu aside, and fell to shouting the name and declaring that the person who had carried off the treasure had been detected. The captain of the guard was convinced that the robbery could have been committed by no one else, and fairly danced with delight at the success of his plan. All the court employés were of the opinion, how-over, that these two had laid their heads together and coached the washerman, and that there was not a particle of truth in the report. As for the vulgar herd, they reasoned that if the party named really had not committed the burglary, how should the washerman know his name? and affirmed stoutly that Subrahmanya was the very scamp who did the business. Everywhere in the village the populace was to be seen in groups discussing the fact that when the magic ointment was used it had turned out that Subrahmanya had stolen the money. The Rajah believed not the story.

When Subrahmanya went home from the court-house that night, the people all along the way pointed their fingers at him with the remark that 'this was the fellow who had committed the burglary.' Ashamed that he had innocently incurred such unjust blame, he went and lay down all alone after eating his meal and began to puzzle his brain over the matter as follows:

'Who could it be that dug the hole in the wall? No one would undertake so daring a deed single-handed. There certainly could not have been less than two or three to pierce so strong a wall. Who could those three be? They must have known the lay of the fort, or they could not have managed so well. When Niladrirajah got me to draw that plan of the fort a few days ago, he asked two or three times about the treasury. What was his purpose in asking such questions? He must be connected in some way or other with the burglary. He asked the height of the wall, too. If he had no connection with the robbery, of what use would the height of the wall be to him? And besides that, before a breath of the matter got abroad in the town, when I was going to the outskirts of the village just at daybreak, he called me and said it was rumoured that burglars had broken into the palace. If he was not one of the gang, how did he know that fact so early in the morning? When I came home that evening, too, I saw him standing in the street. His conduct then was suspicious. Considering all these coincidences, I have no hesitation in pronouncing him the leader of the gang. To-morrow I'll ask the Rajah for an escort of constables, make a descent upon his house without any-one knowing it, and search all the boxes and other receptacles where money is likely to be found. In this way I shall be sure to get a part of the treasure at least. That will free me from blame, at all events.'

Racked by such thoughts as these he dragged wearily through the night, and as soon as it became light paid his respects to the Rajah. He had done nothing, he said, to incur the slightest blame; but if His Highness would intrust him with a few constables and bid them do as he directed, he would assuredly apprehend the thieves with their booty. The Rajah listened attentively to what he had to say, and at once summoned ten constables and charged them straitly to do whatever Subrahmanya should bid them, and to report the result to him. With these men Subrahmanya proceeded direct to the house of Niladri-rajah, and finding the street door closed, stationed a guard around the building and entered the garden by a wicket, with two constables. He found Niladri-rajah in the yard, who, on seeing strangers enter, was much embarrassed.

'Pray, Subrahmanya, on what business have you come here so early in the morning?' asked he.

Simply to visit your honour. What are you having done in the garden?'

'I've been having the garden dug up with the intention of planting it. I was just considering what seed I should sow when you came in,' replied Niladri-rajah, forgetting in his confusion to apply the plural number to himself, and speaking as became his true standing. Without a word Subrahmanya effected an entrance with his men and opened and examined all the boxes. To his astonishment he found in them along with other things the articles which the *byragi* had some time before stolen from his father's house. But not a trace was there of the Rajah's property. Having found his own money, Subrahmanya concluded that the thief could be none other than Niladri-rajah; and guessing that he had buried the articles in the ground and dug the whole garden over to hide all trace of the spot, and then lied in saying that it was for the purpose of sowing seed, he had the constables re-dig the entire enclosure. There in a certain spot, waist-deep in the earth, they came upon the whole of the property lost by the Rajah. Not a *cowrie's* worth was missing. Appointing constables to fetch the treasure round by means of coolies, and to bring along Niladri-rajah and his servants under arrest without delay, Subrahmanya hurried on the palace where he related fully what had occurred, ordered in the baskets of treasure, and handed over the thieves. Niladri-rajah and his accomplices confessed their guilt and begged to be let off. So pleased was the Rajah that he at once rewarded Subrahmanya handsomely; and since, being a tributary vassal of the Peddapuram Rajah, he did not possess the power to try the prisoners, he made them over to the custody of the royal police, appointed Subrahmanya captain of the corps, and despatched them to H. H. Krishna Jagapati, the Maharajah of Peddapuram, for trial.

When Subrahmanya was setting out on his journey to Peddapuram, just as he reached the street door, a poor lizard fell upon him from the ceiling. He immediately postponed his departure, and summoned the village priest to ascertain the consequences of the lizard's fall. This personage soon bustled in, palm leaf *almanac* in hand, and announced that as the reptile had not fallen on his head, his life was in no danger; and further stated that if he would bathe, offer a lighted lamp, and give a little gold to some Brahman or other, no ill effects would result from the fall of the lizard. Subrahmanya at once took a full bath, placed a few coppers in the hands of the priest himself with the remark that copper contained gold, repeated the *gayatri*,* and set out with the determination of reaching Peddapuram that day how hot soever it might be.

* The chief Brahminical *mantra* or incantation, which is supposed to possess peculiar efficacy.

CHAPTER XII.

Ramarajah, with the assistance of Subbarayadu, brings back Sita—Ramarajah finds Rajasekhara in Prison—Rajasekhara's Release from Confinement—Sobhanadri-rajah is Punished—Subbarayadu proves to be Rukmini, and relates her Adventures.

AT a distance of ten or twelve miles from Peddapuram is a village called Jaggampeta. At high noon of the day on which Sita was abducted, two persons came to the house of the *karanam* of this village and shouted to the inmates to open the door. At the summons a strikingly handsome lad of fourteen summers, who for some reason wore his hair long came from within, and, opening the door, demanded on what errand they had come. One of the two men at the door replied by asking whether they would for money give some food to a Brahman girl. On coming out the lad beheld a child of about eight years sitting on the *pial* with downcast eyes, sobbing convulsively. One of the men stood close beside her trying to terrify her into silence. Observing the lad who had just come from the house examining their countenances in a peculiar manner, the men asked him his name.

'Subbarayadu,' he replied; and after studying the child's face closely for a few moments, asked 'Who is this little girl? Where did you bring her from? and where are you taking her to?'

'We live in Cocanada. This child is the daughter of our village *karanam*. Her name's Sitama. She's been staying with her sister in Peddapuram, and we're taking her home to her father's. She's setting up her tune because she doesn't want to come with us.'

'No, no,' interrupted Sita, 'these men are carrying me off.'

'This is certainly not the road from Peddapuram to Cocanada,' remarked Subbarayadu; 'it looks as though what the little girl says is the truth.'

While this dialogue was going on, someone suddenly ran up behind and seized the fellow who stood by Sita's

side by the *juttu*, pulling him down and showering a
rattling fusilade of blows upon his back. The second
man seeing this, deserted Sita and his comrade and
displayed all the agility he possessed in running away.
The individual who had just arrived shouted 'Don't
let him escape! Don't let him escape!' and released
the fellow he had hold of to pursue him who was running away. The second one perceiving this to be his
chance fled in the opposite direction, and showed himself to be the better man of the two. After he had
pursued this man for some distance the stranger returned to the place where Sita sat. No sooner did she
see him than she cried out,

'Oh, Ramarajah! How good of you to deliver me
from the hands of those thieves. Won't you take me
home to my mother, too?'

'Don't cry, dear; I'll set you down at home ere sundown.'

'Rajah,' asked Subbarayadu, 'where are this little
one's parents? They long regarded me as their own
child?'

'If that's so, do you know this little girl?'

'I do. She's Rajasekhara's second daughter. This
little girl, myself, and her elder brother used to regard
one another as brothers and sisters. Her elder sister
and I, especially, were so intimate that we scarcely
knew each other apart. This little one has forgotten
me, I think.'

'The child's parents are now in Bhimavaram. If you
are so deeply indebted to their kindness, why not come
along with me and take the girl to her people?'

'I'll come at all odds. Stay here a moment until I
run into the house and tell our people of my intention
and return,' said Subbarayadu, as he disappeared within.
There he related the whole story, saying that he would
set the child down safely in Bhimavaram and return as
quickly as possible. Although the whole family protested strongly against this, he refused to listen to
them; whereupon they accompanied him to the street

door and saw him off, with many affectionate charges
that he was to hurry back. Ramarajah, astonished at
the lad's beauty, thought within himself how delightful
it would be were such loveliness only found in woman.
As soon as the object of his thoughts appeared,
Ramarajah lifted the little girl upon his shoulder and
took the road for Bhimavaram, conversing with Subbarayadu.

'It's very singular,' said he, 'that you, a Brahman,
wear your hair so long.'

'I'm under a vow to Venkatesvara. On the strength
of that vow I do not remove the coat and other
garments I have on, even at meal times. When my
clothes get soiled I put on clean ones in some room,
with the utmost secrecy, without anyone knowing it.
By the help of God I've kept this vow unbroken up to
the present moment.'

'Your vow is a most singular one. I never heard of
or saw one like it before.'

Chatting in this manner, they reached a small village,
near Bhimavaram, a couple of hours after lamplight.
As the road beyond was in a bad condition, and they
heard that a large tiger had carried off a man just outside the village a couple of days before, Ramarajah
concluded that it would not be judicious to take them
farther in the dark, and found them a lodging for the
night at the house of a farmer in the place. There were
no Brahmans in the village, so they got no dinner that
night. But Ramarajah went to the house of a merchant
and procured some parched rice; and as the people at
whose house they lay kept cows, he begged of them a
dish of thick buttermilk, and gave it to his companions.
After appeasing their hunger somewhat with this frugal
fare, they lay down upon a rush mat supplied by their
host, and were soon wrapped in profound slumber.
Rousing them a good three hours before daylight,
Ramajarah conducted the party on their way to Bhimavaram; but just as they reached the outskirts of the
village, he pretended to have suddenly recollected some

business of importance that he had up to that moment entirely forgotten, and informing his companions that he had some work on hand that must be attended to at once, showed them the road, and hurried off by a side path.

The pair inquired the way for some little distance together; but as soon as Sita reached a street that she knew, she started on a run, leaving Subbarayadu behind, and, turning into an alley, made straight for home. Unable in the dark to discover which alley Sita had entered, Subbarayadu walked straight on to the main street and wandered about the town, unable to find the house. On reaching the street door of her father's house, Sita called to those within, and Manikyamba, who was lying awake upon her couch, unable to sleep for sorrow, started up and came running to open the door. Immediately Sita rushed into her mother's arms and burst into tears. Manikyamba, too, unable to restrain her tears, wept for a while; then wiped away the drops from her daughter's eyes with the end of her cloth, and asked where she had been since yesterday, and how she had been able to return alone in the dark. Sita told her how, early the previous morning, two kidnappers had carried her off; how Ramarajah and another young man had rescued her and brought her back; and how Ramarajah had left them, just at the entrance to the village, on the plea of having some business to attend to. But what, asked Manikyamba anxiously, had become of the other young man? The daughter replied that he had accompanied her as far as the next street; that he was a person who had known them all before; and that he would be along shortly. While Manikyamba was thus talking with Sita, who was perched upon her knee, it became daylight. Just then someone at the street door asked 'where Rajasekhara's house was.' Manikyamba overheard the inquiry, and thinking the voice sounded like Rukmini's, she put Sita down from her lap, reached the street door at a bound, and cried out, 'Who's there?' The moment Subbarayadu caught sight of

her, he cried 'mother!' and falling on her neck, began
to sob aloud. A moment later the three disappeared
within.

While Rajesekhara, the same day he was thrown into
prison, was sitting sorrowfully apart, a convict, past the
prime of life, shuffled by in his fetters, and, after gazing
a moment into Rajasekhara's face, approached him and
sat down.

'What's your name?' asked Rajasekhara.

'My name's Papayya,' replied the convict; 'our
family name is Manchirajah. Have you any recollection of ever seeing me before?'

'Your face certainly does look as though I had seen
it somewhere before; but I can't for the life of me
think where it was. What relation is Manchirajah
Padmarajah to you?'

'You saw me under the *juvvi* tree at Black Lake. I
was then disguised as a *byragi*, and so you have failed
to recognize me. Padmarajah is my son.'

'By what turn of fortune have you been reduced from
your former position to such a state as this, and in so
short a time?'

'Through the mistake of making friends with this
Sobhanadri-rajah I fell into his power. This Rajah gave
me four mates and made me their captain, and sent us
to the Black Lake to plunder the roads. After the
hillsman, Ramareddi, and his gang were captured and
hanged to the branches of the trees by the Rajah, we
had it all to ourselves, and for two months were famous
for our highway robberies. Sobhanadri-rajah got half the
booty; half of the remaining half fell to my share; while a
quarter of the sum total was divided among themselves
by the four other fellows. I palmed myself off as a
yogi. My companions spent the day at a distance in
the jungle, and came in at night to get their instruc-
tions. When it was necessary to send them any
message by day, I despatched the mountaineer who lived
in the hut. I paid him myself, independent of the
others.'

'He's the one, isn't he, who took his bow and arrows and came with me that day ?'

'Yes; the pot-bellied chap's the very one. On the very night I sent them after you, one of the four was killed. The Rajah got wind of it somehow, and the next morning, before daylight, along came the Royal police, and, first of all, seized me and the mountaineer. Then they beat the hillsman, and he disclosed where the others were hid; so they captured them, too, and brought the whole lot of us to the Rajah. He threw us all into prison. There we were punished, of course; but we didn't split on our Rajah for all that. So he allows us to go about as we please in prison here, and regards us with special favour.'

'In that case Sobhanadri-rajah is doing you a great kindness.'

'What kindness? It is through this villain that we are suffering here in goal. But, sooner or later, the Maharajah will discover his villany, and consign him to this beautiful abode to keep us company. Then, when another gaolor comes, the Lord only knows what we'll have to undergo.'

''Twas for no other reason than because I wouldn't give my daughter to your son, I'd have you know, that he put me in here.'

'Yes; I know all about it. Padmarajah was here with me that time the Rajah sent to call him when you were with him. The whole thing was a plan arranged by me, my son, the Rajah, and the astrologer together. But your days are lucky, and so our little plan didn't succeed. Sobhanadri-rajah intended taking the chains off two of the fellows who used to be with me at Black Lake, and send them somewhere this morning.'

'Did you not learn where to?'

'No; I didn't find out. This morning the Rajah came here to consult me about something, but his younger brother happened in, and so he moved off, saying he'd tell me to-night. A while ago I did you a great wrong; now I'll make it even by doing you a right. The Maharajah of Peddapuram is a most excellent man. If you were to write a petition to the effect that Sobhanadri-rajah is keeping you confined in this way, he'd release you instanter. I'll fetch you paper and that;' and Papayya, as good as his word, soon returned with the necessary writing materials. Without delay Rajasekhara wrote a petition, which he folded and gummed and handed to Papayya, who sent it by a special messenger to the Maharajah. Two or three days passed away, but no order nor any sign that he would grant Rajasekhara a trial and justice came from the Rajah. Rajasekhara concluded that, as it was a charge against a relative of the Rajah's, no reply would be forthcoming, and dismissed the matter from his thoughts.

Early on the morning of the day after Sita was kidnapped, a rumour got afloat in the prison that the Maharajah was coming to inspect the premises. A little later Ramarajah came into the cell where Rajasekhara was confined.

'Ramarajah,' cried Rajasekhara, 'you must forgive my blunder. Your bringing the letter that night proved a blessing in disguise to us. I was unable to see through the affair at the time, and abused you unjustly.'

'It's time you said so in return for the service I did you. You evinced such good sense as almost to prevent me ever doing a charitable deed again!'

'Be merciful to me and forget that matter, I beg. I was beside myself at the time at the thought that we had missed a capital match, and said I know not what. Forgive me.'

'They say the Maharajah is on his way here to inspect the prison, so I must be off at once,' said Ramarajah as he took his departure.

About an hour later a be-badged attendant entered the cell, and bade Rajasekhara follow him, saying that the Maharajah was holding court, and had summoned Rajasekhara because of a certain petition he had written. Arrived at the hall, Rajasekhara beheld the Maharajah seated upon a jewelled throne, decked in all his regalia.

In the royal presence stood the lictors, bearing in their hands golden *fasces*. At the sides of the throne were two attendants waving rich *chowries* or fans; and a bodyguard fully armed. On one side stood Sobhanadri-rajah, with clasped hands; on the other, two other men, whose hands were bound. When Rajasekhara at last stood before him, the Maharajah Krishna Jagapati asked if he had not written a petition in the royal name against Sobhanadri-rajah, there present. Rajasekhara, fearful of the consequences of his act, and trembling in every limb, remained mute, unable to answer a word.

'Sobhanadri-rajah,' proceeded his Highness, 'we happen to know of the many injustices you have done Rajasekhara here. Simply because he refused to sacrifice his daughter to a base wretch, one of your familiars, you not only cast him into prison, but called to your aid, and instigated two men from the prison to abduct the child.

'I know nothing whatever about the persons who abducted the child your Highness speaks of,' replied Sobhanadri-rajah.

'If you have no knowledge of the matter, how did these men, who were yesterday in the prison, succeed in getting out?'

'Yesterday morning these fellows scaled the wall, and escaped. Ever since then I have been sending men in all directions for their apprehension.'

'What you, Guravu! Did this man send you anywhere, or did you effect your escape yourselves by scaling the wall?'

'Most gracious master, yesterday his honour the Rajah, here, summoned us, and bade us carry off the girl to Ravanakkapeta, and there deliver her to Padma-rajah. Padmarajah went on ahead, and was waiting there to marry the girl underhanded as soon as she arrived.'

'No, no,' broke in Sobhanadri-rajah; 'these low-born thieves ran off, and are lying in this way to shield themselves.'

'This Rajah's the ringleader of the thieves!' proceeded Guravu excitedly; 'he used to get us to rob the roads, and then wouldn't give us our pay properly, and got us into all sorts of scrapes. It grieves me merely to think of what we suffered the night we tried to rob this brahman.'

'Did you use to rob the roads as he says?' demanded the Maharajah, turning to Sobhanadri-rajah.

'Never, never! These sons of widows are lying.'

'Call Papayya, and see whether what we've said isn't true. He's close by in the prison here.'

'Call Papayya there,' commanded the Rajah.

After a little, in came Papayya, and on the Maharajah giving his word that his punishment would be materially diminished if he spake the truth, he narrated the whole affair, from the very beginning. Sobhanadri-rajah gazed at the floor in silence, unable to utter a word in reply. Rajasekhara, observing that the Maharajah's features and form bore a remarkable resemblance to those of Ramarajah, broke into a cold sweat, and gazed about him, pale and bewildered. His Highness marked his pallor and agitation, and descending from the throne took him graciously by the hand, and explained that he who had so often come to their house to inquire after their welfare was no other than himself, and that although well able to help them, he had delayed doing so for a while in order to put their character to the test. He then turned to his attendants and ordered Rajasekhara's immediate release. For a few moments Rajasekhara was unable to collect his thoughts sufficiently to reply; but as his fear wore off he gradually found voice, and prayed in quavering accents, and with deep humility, that 'His lord would forgive him for regarding him as a common man, and treating him with disrespect through ignorance of his real estate, and for uttering abusive words when angry that Sita's marriage had been frustrated.' His Highness replied that the matter had never presented itself to him in any other light than that, and after graciously inviting Rajasekhara to visit him the next day in Peddapuram, sent him home.

After Rajasekhara's departure, the Maharajah summoned Sobhanadri-rajah, recounted at length his evil deeds, and reprimanded him severely. Although for his crimes he should have been condemned to a punishment of unusual rigour, the Rajah with excessive leniency assigned him only a month's imprisonment, and handed him over to the custody of the constables. Besides this, since he had promised the two men who carried Sita off, when he had himself captured and brought them back, that their punishment should be somewhat lessened if they would tell the whole truth, he not only diminished their sentence by half, but was equally lenient to Padmarajah. Having disposed of this business, Sri Krishna Jagapati Maharajah mounted a superb elephant, and, amid the panegyrics and plaudits of his heralds and bards, the rolling of drums and tabrets, and the braying of wind instruments, proceeded in state to his capital, attended by all his regal retinue.

When Rajasekhara reached home, Manikyamba was sitting leaning against the wall of the west room, talking to Subbarayadu, with downcast head. On reaching the street-door, Rajasekhara perceived with astonishment that the lad's features, as well as his voice, resembled those of Rukmini; but, observing the lad to be in male attire, he knew not what to think, and instead of entering the house, stood rooted to the spot, gazing fixedly in his perplexity at the lad's face. Just then Sita peeped out of doors, and shouting, 'Oh, mother! papa's come,' ran to her father and embraced him.

Filled with the utmost delight at the news, Manikyamba rose immediately, and brought water and laved her husband's feet, wiped them dry with the end of her cloth, and placed a stool near the wall for him to sit upon. Seating himself on this, Rajasekhara kissed Sita, and took her upon his knee. Then Manikyamba told him how kidnappers had carried Sita off, and how Ramarajah and another lad had rescued her and brought her back. Rajasekhara in turn told them that Ramarajah was the Maharajah Krishna Jagapati, sovereign ruler of Peddapuram; that he was in the habit of going about in disguise to acquaint himself with the condition of his subjects; and that, coming to them under the name Ramarajah, he had done them a great kindness, and had, to crown all, just released him from prison. Then he related the events which had led to his deliverance, and expatiated at length on the admirable qualities of their sovereign lord. Manikyamba's astonishment knew no bounds when she heard that Ramarajah was their Rajah; and she lauded his lack of pride and magnanimity of disposition to the skies.

In the very midst of this conversation, Subbarayadu approached and fell at Rajasekhara's feet with the exclamation, 'I am Rukmini.' Unable for a moment to speak for excessive joy, he at length calmed himself and arose and embraced his long lost daughter. The parents' joy at the restoration of one whom they had mourned as dead was too great for description. At such a moment they were wholly unable to restrain their feelings; but after the vehemence of their emotion had somewhat subsided, they begged Rukmini to relate to them all that had befallen her from the day she left them up to that moment. The story of her adventures Rukmini then proceeded to tell as follows:

'When I came to myself and looked about me the night the robbers attacked us, the moon was shining brightly, and the whole surface of the clearing shone as though flour had been spread over it to dry—but, to my horror, I lay stretched upon the bare earth in the midst of the jungle. Peer about me as I would on every hand, not a human form could I discern anywhere. Not a trace of man was to be seen, and only the roaring of wild beasts fell upon my ears. Just then a tiger sprang from the thicket close beside me, but without seeing me, and dragged off the trunk of a man which lay near. At the sight I fainted away, but after I had partially regained consciousness, I noticed

that none of you were near, and believing that if you
were alive you would not leave me alone in such a
place, I concluded that you had been killed by the
robbers, and that the wild beasts had made away with
your bodies; and having no friend to whom to look
nor god to whom to pray, I resolved to seek death.
Then the thought occurred to me that self-destruction
is sin; and thinking that perhaps some of you might
still be alive and that I might again be blessed with a
sight of you, I abandoned the attempt to take my life,
and rose to my feet and walked a few steps. Just then
I caught sight of a head lying near smeared with gore,
and a bundle of clothes close beside it. Although in
such imminent peril of my life I was tormented by an
unendurable hunger, and, picking up the bundle, I
opened it and examined the contents in hope of finding
something to eat. But it contained only clothes such as
men wear. No sooner did I see these than it occurred
to me that it was unsafe for a good-looking woman
to go about alone undisguised, and that I might reach
some village in safety by assuming man's dress. So I
put on the clothes, including the coat, and soon stood
in complete male costume. My own clothes I tied in
a bundle with what remained in the one I had found,
took off all the jewelry I had upon my person, tied it in
a corner of my cloth, and started. After following a
footpath until daybreak, I reached a village. Here I
remained a day, obtained a little money by selling my
jewels, and then, though in terrible agony from the
wound in my head, went on to another village near.
In this place I stopped several days for the sake of
medical assistance. After getting a little better I
started again, and after wandering about in all the
villages of that vicinity and taking my meals at inns,
about ten days ago I reached Jaggampeta. The *karanam*
of the place was old and without a son. He took a
fancy to me as soon as he saw me, and thinking that I
might be helpful to him in his work, he made me welcome to his home. He was greatly pleased with my

behaviour, and inquired my caste and family with the intention of marrying his only daughter to me and of keeping me permanently by him. I assumed the name of Subbarayadu, and while there remained faithful to my benefactors and assisted in the writing of accounts and other papers by means of the education you had given me. I told them that my people had made me wear my hair long because of a vow to Venkatesvara—that I must not anoint my head until that vow was fulfilled—and that I was not to change the clothes I wore in the presence of others. I got them to agree to help me preserve my vow inviolate, and exercised the greatest caution that my disguise might not be penetrated.

'While things were moving on in this way, one day at noon a couple of men brought Sita to the house where I lived and asked us to give them a meal. Just then the Rajah to whom we gave water and saved his life, came up and beat them and drove them away. So I took leave of the people of the house, and, with the Rajah, brought Sita back home. All along the road I thought I wouldn't tell any of you that I was Rukmini until you recognised me and found it out for yourselves. But when I saw mother I couldn't restrain myself. My grief overflowed, and I clasped her in my arms and let the whole secret out.'

When Rukmini had finished this narrative, Rajasekhara, vastly pleased at his daughter's sense and bravery, took her to his heart and caressed her fondly.

Let none who read this story of Rukmini declare it impossible to believe the statement that a mere girl of fourteen summers, who had lived so dutiful a daughter as never to cross the threshold of her home nor set foot even in the next street of her own village, could resort to a device so indicative of courage and good sense, assume so impenetrable a disguise, and maintain her incognito in a manner most difficult, even for women of mature age and long experience in the ways of the world. Let who will believe, or disbelieve; since it is the duty of the historian to speak the truth without qualification, I narrate the event as it occurred. This book contains no impossible tales of men assuming the forms of deer, or of their being completely metamorphosed into women, as in the *puranic* fables. Her preceptress in such extraordinary conduct was none other than Sarasvati* herself whose protection she sought. And who that knows the power of education, will express surprise at this as being a remarkable performance ?

CHAPTER XIII.

Sankarayya arrives with the Coin Necklace—He relates his Father's Misadventure—Procession of the Vaishnava *gurus*—The Return of Nrusimhaswami—He relates his Story.

WHILE Rukmini and her parents were conversing in the manner related above, a lad of some fourteen summers came in, and throwing aside the bundle of cloths he carried on his shoulder, fell at Rajasekhara's feet with the exclamation 'Alas, father-in-law!' and burst into tears.

'What, Sankarayya,' remonstrated Rajasekhara; 'crying like a girl! Shut up.'

'My father died fifteen years ago,' sobbed the lad, 'and I wasn't at home at the time, either.'

'What did he die of? and where were you that you were not in the place then?'

'He did not die a natural death. He came to his end through the burning down of the house. As much as ten days before it happened I had taken my stepmother to Ellore. While I was there I got the news of his death.'

'Tell me fully how the house was burned, and why he was unable to leave it.'

'While you were still in the village, my father was celebrated for his witch-doctoring, you remember. Afterwards his fame spread in the surrounding villages as well. If in any house anyone so much as got a

* The Goddess of Wisdom.

little fever, they'd call my father to administer holy water. If anyone but had a twinge in his toe, he'd get father to apply an amulet. If any person was thought possessed, father was called in. If anyone but got afraid, he'd have father apply sacred ashes. In short, it mattered not what the complaint was, among all the villages of the vicinity there wasn't a single one to which they didn't summon father. For this reason people brought all sorts of articles to our house and presented them to father with the most implicit faith in his healing powers. No matter in whose house any festivity took place, the first gift was always father's.

'Things moved on in this way for some time. One morning, while father was walking along the street, he saw by a toddy-drawer's door a cocoa-nut tree loaded with bunches of green fruit. He called the owner of the house and asked him to send around a few tender nuts in the husk. The fellow was an impudent prig, and replied that when father fetched the money for the nuts he'd get them. At this father flew into a terrible rage, and abused the fellow right roundly because he wouldn't give him the nuts. "I'll give you no nuts; but I'll look out for what you'll do to me in your spite," declared the toddy-drawer, not yielding an inch. "Look out for your tree—see what'll happen to it by this time to-morrow," cried father, with a significant shake of his head as he turned away and walked home. "Oh," replied the other, as he went into the house, "I'll not forget your threat to raise fiends and kill it."

'About twelve o'clock that night my father woke me out of a sound sleep, and bidding me tie up a gill of rice in the end of my cloth and fetch the washing cup along in my hand, he started out into the dark and bade me follow him. It was the dead of night, and so dark that you couldn't see your hand before you. But by feeling our way along we at last reached the toddy-drawer's house, where we stopped. Telling me to stay there a moment, my father fastened a strap to his feet, and speeling up the cocoa-nut tree, smashed open the young shoot with a stick, poured into it the rice and water I had brought, and came down as noiselessly as he went up. When we reached home again it was midnight, and my father laid down and enjoyed a sound sleep. The next day he began to announce to everybody who came to the house " that he had bewitched the toddy-man's cocoa-nut tree, because he had refused him some nuts." To support his assertion, from that very day the root shrivelled, the leaves withered, and in five or six days the tree died. The toddy-drawer then began to raise a row, and to inform everybody " that the Brahman had got mad at him because he wouldn't give him some green nuts, and had, without any reason whatever, bewitched his tree and killed it." In a very short time this report spread to the adjacent villages, and on the strength of it all the people began to regard my father with suspicion.

'A little later someone in the place fell sick, and some suspected that my father had bewitched him. So, when the townsfolk had any sickness in their houses, they ceased calling my father as frequently as before. Yet in their hearts they feared what he might do if they didn't call him. In the meantime a merchant's child fell ill, and his mother and great grandmother went and consulted an oracle. The Pariah woman, who had charge of the Temple of Pārantāla, thereupon declared that someone in the place had bewitched the child. So the two of them came home crying and told the men the whole story. They at once came to the conclusion that the person who had bewitched the child was, without doubt, my father, and called in witch doctors, and did their very best to cure the young one. But they didn't happen to hit upon the right prescription for the disease under treatment; and, besides, the witch doctors took to giving the child frequent baths while the fever was at its height, and so the lad gave up the ghost and paid the debt of nature. From that time all the villagers were possessed with the notion that my father was bewitching and killing everybody. As an aid to the spread of this illusion, two old widows of the place took to impersonating those who had before died in the village, and shrieking that they had come to their end through witchcraft, and that their folk, unable to discover the true state of their case, had been deceived into thinking them sick, and so had lost them. Besides this, Kamesvara and other household gods inspired the widows of several families, who began to declare when anyone fell ill that it was the effect of enchantment. For these reasons, no matter who was taken down with disease in the place, the people were deluded into believing the whole thing to be simply the result of my father's incantations. It mattered not that father averred again and again upon his oath that he was wholly innocent of any fault; there was not one who credited his asseverations. It was simply impossible to describe the craze that took possession of the people! They believed for a certainty that all who died in the place came to their end by my father's enchantments. All the invalids, they thought, were suffering from no other cause than my father's magic power. In consequence, the villagers in a little while came to regard father as a sort of local death-god. Whenever he showed his face, the females of the place fell to reviling him and snapping their fingers at him in derision. The men, with angry looks, gave him the cold shoulder, and, as soon as he appeared, got out of the way and slipped down the back alleys. The neighbours even stopped giving him live coals with which to start his fires. If he went to borrow anything, they replied they hadn't got it. Those who lived next door, absolutely declined to allow him to draw water from their well. Living thus in the very midst of the enemy became most trying to poor father; but knowing that the whole affair was undoubtedly the evil fruit of his assuming the guise of a witch doctor, he bore it all without the least sign of regret, or grumbling at the consequence of his own guilt. One day, while matters were in this condition, my stepmother fell sick; and, notwithstanding our most earnest entreaties, not one was there in the place who would come to give her nourishment and drink, or to stand by and talk to her to prevent her falling asleep. None of the villagers would so much as allow us to fetch water from their wells for cooking and drinking. It was only the fourth day after you left the place that Nambi Varudacharya, who had so long acted as village doctor, died. You remember after you dismissed Nati Ramayya for stealing the two copper drinking cups and giving them to the prostitute while working as Brahman cook in our house, that he lived by keeping school, since he was good for nothing else in the world? Well, no sooner did Varudacharya die, than this fellow began the practice of medicine as well, and he's now the most celebrated physician in the place. When he first began to practice he was a new hand, so he used to get my father himself to write down for him the names of diseases and of drugs. He would sort the latter into red and black vials and fetch them to father, to ascertain what colour belonged to a certain medicine, when he would label them "Rise of the Full Moon," "Rheumatic Eradicator," and the like. In our house, too, he prepared his pills, mixing red lead with such substances as cummin, fennel, and black pepper, and reducing them with lime juice. It mattered not what medicine you wanted; he'd never say he hadn't it in stock, but would hand it over at the modest charge of from one to twenty rupees per ounce. Of the money he made at the commencement of his practice, he gave my father a share; but after he had acquired the reputation of being a great physician, when my father fell out with the people of the place, he ceased giving this. Though father afterwards went in person and begged him to come and see his sick wife, he was so mean a fellow that, through fear of the populace, he wouldn't call even once. The truth is, the villagers gave all the trouble that lay in their power. They began to shower clods of earth upon the roof after dark. Leaving me to look after his wife, father would go to the tank, and, after having his bath, fetch the water, prepare the food, and give her some nourishment by midday, worrying himself nearly to death in the meantime over the kindnesses you had done him, and the fact that, were you in the place, he would certainly not suffer such persecution. After prolonged sufferings mother-in-law got somewhat better, but for some reason did not seem to regain her proper strength. The opposition of the villagers grew worse and worse. By the time we looked out of a morning, our doorway was usually heaped with dirty rubbish and human skulls. These my father would remove, bathing two or three times a day. And as his wife hadn't proper attention there, he placed her under my care and sent her to her home in Hailpuram in a palanquin, remaining behind himself to look after the house.

'On the night of the day after we started, about two hours after dark, we arrived safely in Ellore. Here the food and cooking agreed with my mother. Her parents, too, showed her every kindness; and in a very short time she became convalescent. One day my stepmother's brother and I were sitting on a *pial*, some two feet high, built in the form of a circle about a *ravi* tree in the street—my stepmother's father had married a *ravi* and a *margosa*, you see, and had built this great *pial* around them—the village *karanam* always transacted his business on this *pial* in the shade of the tree. Well, one morning while we were sitting here cleaning our teeth, up came a dark-complexioned Sudra, about thirty years of age, dressed in white clothes, and with a bundle stuck under his arm, and asked, "would we buy a coin necklace?" Where is it?" asked my uncle; "let us see it." The Sudra sat down on the *pial*, and, opening his bundle, produced a necklace, which he handed to my uncle. After examining it, he asked the price, and handed it over to me to see whether it was of value or not. No sooner had I taken it in my hand and examined it, than I recognized it as Rukmini's by the big gem. "Where did you get this?" I asked.

"I am a trader," he replied, "and had a workman in my native place weave it with silk." At that I asserted that the necklace belonged to a relative of mine; "and as you have stolen goods on you, I'll hand you over to the police," I added, to frighten him. But he manifested not the slightest fear. He dashed the necklace down at our feet, and went off crying that " he'd go to the station and enter a complaint against us, and bring the constables and have us arrested." I stayed in the place two whole days longer, but I saw nothing more of him.

'Early on the morning of the third day after this event a cooly arrived from Dhavalesvaram with a letter for me, sent by Ramamurti. On opening and reading it I learned the sad news that on that very day father's house had taken fire, and that he had been burned to death. I was to come as quick as possible, the letter added. Heartbroken at this intelligence, for it was sudden as a thunder-clap, I went into the house weeping, and communicated the bad news to my stepmother. No sooner did she hear it than she fell upon the floor and began to roll about with dishevelled hair, thumping her bosom, and shrieking like to lift the roof. After her shrieks and sobs had somewhat abated I consoled her as well as I could, and taking the cooly along with me started at once. I walked so hard until dawn the following morning that I blistered my feet, but finally reached home at midday. Of the house, nothing remained but the bare walls. Strange to say, not one of the adjoining houses had been touched—ours alone falling a prey to Parasu Rama. While I was standing gazing at the ruins, some of the neighbours came up and sought to console me. Four days before, they said, the house had suddenly caught fire in the night, and ere assistance could arrive, had burned to the ground. I then went to Narayanamurti's house. Ever since you left the place my father and Narayanamurti had been bosom friends. A month after you left Dhavalesvaram thieves broke into Narayanamurti's house and robbed

him of his entire fortune in a single night. He was
thus again reduced to poverty, and began to court my
father's favour. Father sent him about as an assistant
in his practice, and gave him in return a small allow-
ance for his meals. When the villagers became father's
enemies, Narayanamurti alone remained faithful to him.
Your brother-in-law now became afraid that the villagers
would rob his house; so one night, bidding me accompany him, he carried the box containing his jewels and
cash secretly to Narayanamurti's house, where he deposited it in his friend's bedroom, sealed it up, and,
locking it with a padlock, retained the key in his own
possession. When Narayanamurti saw me, the thought
of my father's terrible fate rushed upon him, and, over-
come by emotion, he cried: "And the box of jewels
that you deposited with me for safe keeping—you even
had to go and take that away just before your death!"
I went into the bedroom, but no box was to be seen.
Neither could I find a trace of it anywhere in the house.
When I afterwards asked about my father's disease,
Narayanamurti replied that from the time I went to
Hailapuram, your brother-in-law, apprehending that
someone would do him violence if he went into the
street, remained closely indoors; that after this had
gone on for two or three days, a rumour got abroad in
the town "that Damodarayya was sitting in his house
with the doors shut, performing some mysterious Satanic
burnt offering;" that thereupon the whole body of villagers took the matter into consideration and concluded
that he was certainly repeating some diabolical incantation to destroy them all, and called a council on the
banks of the Godaveri in the belief that unless they
could frustrate the effort they were done for; and that
the holocaust of the house and all the other mysterious
circumstances connected with my father's death had
occurred on the same night. I remained at his house
until the ten days' obsequies were at an end, and as it
would not do to start on the 13th, got off on the 14th,
and was making my way with the necklace to the

village where you now live, when the astrologer turned up in the road. He took me aside a little way, and said he had a secret to tell me. After disclosing the fact that Narayanamurti had concealed our box of jewels in his house, he said that if we gave him a hundred rupees he would deliver the box to us instead of to him. He also added that as soon as I returned after seeing my father-in-law, I must enter a charge against Narayanamurti. I replied, "All right," and came on looking for you.'

When Sankarayya had related his father's sad story as above, he untied his bundle, and taking from it a coin necklace, handed it to Rajasekhara. Receiving this, the latter embraced and consoled his nephew, and shed some tears of sorrow at the death of Damodarayya. Then the whole household wailed in concert for a moment for the dead, after which they had their bath and dined. The remainder of the afternoon was spent in telling and hearing news.

Shortly after the lamps were lighted the sound of music was heard, and Rajasekhara and the others went into the street to ascertain what was going on. A Vaishnava priest, coated thickly with the twelve upright marks, and accompanied by two attendants fanning him with huge fans, was seated in a palanquin, proceeding in state through the town amid the flaring of numerous torches. Behind him walked several Telaganyas, and a solitary Vaishnava, all plastered over with sandal-wood paste, and fanning themselves with palm-leaf fans. The Vaishnava Rajasekhara knew; so he called him over to where he was standing, and began conversing with him.

'Aren't you priest to the Gudūris down in Dhavalesvaram?'

'I am. The Avasaralas of this place are disciples of him you see in the palanquin.'

'But when I saw you last, weren't you the priest and he the disciple?'

'We don't recognise any such distinction as that

among us. We change about, d'ye see. Where I've got disciples, he's my disciple; and where he's got disciples, I'm his. His grandfather and mine were brothers. His father, Prativadi-bhayankara Gaudabherundacharya, was unrivalled the world over as a *pandit*. After our grandfathers and fathers had departed to Paradise, we divided the disciples these had made into equal lots. Those in this place fell to me, while those in Dhavalesvaram fell to him. Once a year we leave Sri Kūrmam, where we reside, and go the rounds among our followers after this fashion.'

'You said before, didn't you, that he couldn't read? How does he instruct his disciples?'

'I haven't a whit more education than he's got. What education is necessary to instruct one's disciples? We whisper the *ashtakshari** in their ears, bid them repeat it one hundred and eight times a day, tell them that if they trust and serve their priest as their only god, heaven is ready won, brand them upon the shoulders, and take our gratuity and go our way. We argue with nobody, so everybody considers us *pandits* for certain.'

'Do you propose remaining several days in the place?'

'We shan't stop. We'll be off to-morrow. But I'll call later on and have a chat at leisure,' said he, as he started off on the run to catch the palanquin.

When the procession had passed, the men shut the street door and were about sitting down to their evening meal when some one approached the door and began calling for 'Rajasekhara! Father-in-law!' On Manikyamba's going into the passage and asking who was there, 'I'm Nrusimhaswami,' replied a voice from without. No sooner had Manikyamba heard this statement and the name, then she rushed in terror and told her husband. 'Long as Nrusimhaswami has been dead, he has never even so much as appeared to me in my dreams; what can be the meaning of this enmity now?'

* The 'five-syllabled' *mantra*.

queried she in terrified perplexity. The shouts at the street door were now repeated ; and as Rajasekhara had by this time finished his meal,* he lighted a lamp and started to open the door. When he had done so, sure enough Nrusimhaswami himself seized his hand with the exclamation 'Father-in-law!' He saw his son-in-law plainly enough; but the poor man was unable to believe the evidence of his senses, and examined the new comer's person again and again. After making sure from the fact that the feet were in their proper position and not reversed, that it was no wraith, he led the lad inside, where, telling his wife that it was undoubtedly their Nrusimhaswami come back to them again, he bade them hurry and provide some water for the traveller's feet. Even then it was only after bringing the lamp and examining his face closely that Manikyamba exclaimed 'My poor lad!' and embraced him with tears. Seeing her weep, the son-in-law burst into tears also. After this scene Nrusimhaswami washed his feet, and while eating his meal proceeded to relate the story of his pilgrimage to Kasi, of his friend's deserting him on the way, and other adventures which had befallen him as follows :

'I had long cherished the desire to make the pilgrimage to Kasi, but had abandoned the idea as impracticable for me because of having no suitable companion. But one day the Chamartus boy Seshachalam came along, and after making me give him my word of honour not to tell anyone, confided to me as a secret that he wanted to do penance at the Himalaya mountains and acquire the art of transmuting metals. If I would come along too he would take me with him and teach me the art, and then when the two of us had got the recipe for making gold, we were to return home, manufacture all the gold we wanted, and so become millionaires. Excited by this view of the matter, I conceived a great desire to make at least the attempt; and decided not only to start, but, if possible, to perform the whole journey into

* A Brahmin never finishes an interrupted meal.

the bargain. The two of us talked the matter over secretly in school; and having agreed as to the day on which we should start, spent the intervening time in collecting our clothes and other articles needed in a safe place. Early one morning after breakfast, on the plea that we were going to the *sastri's* to repeat our assignment of verses, we got away, and by keeping straight on reached Peddapuram at sunrise the next morning. The day before that on which we started had been my birthday, and my people had made it a holiday and presented me with a gold collar and bracelets. The same night I had opened my father's chest with a duplicate key and tied up some eighty-four rupees it contained in my pack, and the next day we left the village with these jewels and the cash. Seshachalam had brought with him only three rupees; so all along the way I had to fork out whatever money was needed for the pair of us. By the time we had passed Jagannadham and reached Kattak all the rupees I had by me were spent. There I disposed of my bracelets for forty-two rupees, and by curtailing expenses somewhat managed to make this money do until we reached Kasi. The whole way he kept plaguing me to give him something to spend on his own account, but I would never let him have more than a rupee in his hands at once. At this he became sullen and got down in the mouth and would have nothing to say to me. On the whole he acted very shabbily. When we reached Kasi I still had four rupees left, but in ten days' time this was all gone too. Then I sold my beautiful collar to a trader in Kasi for a hundred and fifty rupees. Instead of making gold as we had at first anticipated, we lost what gold we already possessed. Seshachalam lazied away his time on my money and without the slightest anxiety about his living. But not satisfied with that, even, he came to me one day and said he had occasion for fifty rupees, and would I give them to him? I unfeelingly replied that I wouldn't. This led to a quarrel, and he went off at noon without even so much as touching the food ready served for his dinner, and abusing me as an ingrate. I spent four months more in Kasi. Then I got homesick, and set out and worked my way slowly homewards. Yesterday morning I heard in Tuni that you were here.'

When Nrusimhaswami had made an end of relating his adventures, Rajasekhara told him of the outrageous conduct of Seshachalam,* after which he spread a bed for the weary lad, and, when he had lain down and dropped off to sleep, himself retired to rest.

CHAPTER XIV.

Subrahmanya comes from Pitapuram on a Visit to his Father—The Advent of Sri Sankaracharya—Niladri-rajah relates his Adventures before the Council—Maharajah Krushna Jagapati redeems and restores Rajasekhara's Lands.

SUBRAHMANYA set out from Pitapuram and came in company with the Rajah's constables, who escorted Niladri-rajah, with the money, as far as Bhimavaram, where, directing them to proceed to Peddapuram, he went alone direct to his father's house. When he arrived there, Rajasekhara was just on the point of going to dinner. No sooner did the son set foot inside the street door, than his father caught sight of him and cried, 'The boy has come!' At this all the inmates of the house came running out together, crying: 'Where is he? Where is he?' Sita, however, outran the others, and was first to embrace her brother. Manikyamba next came up and was embraced by her son, who then knelt for his parents' blessing. While this was going on Nrusimhaswami also appeared on the scene, and seized Subrahmanya's hand, with the exclamation, 'hallo, brother-in-law!' Subrahmanya recognized the voice and gazed into his face stupefied, then looked about from one to another of the group inquiringly. After a moment, however, he threw his arms about his

* In announcing that his friend had died by the way.

brother-in-law and asked when he had come; then, recalling his sister's sad fate, exclaimed: ' Alas, that it was not poor Rukmini's lot to have the joy of hearing that her husband lives!' and burst into tears.' Rajasekhara now came forward and consoled the lad, telling him that Rukmini was still alive; and proceeded to relate what dangers had befallen her after that night when they were attacked by highwaymen, and how she had finally reached home in safety. Long before this account of his sister's adventures was complete, Subrahmanya, unable longer to contain his joy, rushed into the room and embraced his sister, and, on her beginning to weep at sight of him, comforted her in turn. When he returned, Nrusimhaswami gave him a long account of his adventures. Then all had their bath and sat down to their meal in new-washed cloths. During the dinner Subrahmanya told the wondering company of the burglary in the Rajah's palace at Pitapuram; how he himself had caught the robbers; how that among the articles recovered he had discovered their lost treasure carried off along ago by the *byragi*; and how he had been put in charge of the thieves who were sent to the Maharajah Krushna Jagapati for trial. He also added that the Pitapuram Rajah had promised him a capital situation as soon as he returned to that place. 'Why!' burst in Rajasekhara, ' the Ramarajah who used to come and go about our house is this very same Maharajah Krushna Jagapati;' and he proceeded to inform his son of the Rajah's remarkable conduct and of the kindness he had shown him, and spoke of their benefactor in terms of the highest praise. Dinner was now at an end; so they rose and washed their hands, had their betel and leaf, and put on clean cloths, when Rajasekhara and Subrahmanya took Nrusimhaswami along and set out on their way to Peddapuram.

On reaching Peddapuram they were just about entering the main street, when, at a little distance, they espied a palanquin, preceded by an elephant, two horses, a huge kettle-drum mounted upon a cart, with

12—2

other musical instruments, and, close behind, a multitude of followers. Seeing the procession, Rajasekhara supposed there must be some religious pageant in progress that day, and, turning to his son, asked whose feast it was, ' Siva's or Vishnu's ?'

'This is not a religious festival,' replied Subrahmanya; 'Sri Sankara Bhagavatpadula is visiting the town. He spent ten days in Peddapuram. Just as I was coming away I noticed that he had bandies and everything ready at the house for the journey to this place.'

'Did the contributions amount to much there ?'

'They footed up right handsomely. The priest sent pastoral letters to each house and collected money at the rate of a rupee a head. Besides this, lots of widows and rich folk used to go with trays of fruit and rupees and offer them for the sake of the privilege of worshipping his feet. Whenever they prostrated themselves at full length, the Swami would say " Narayana !" while the disciples who stood near whisked away the contents of the trays and returned them empty to their owners. The Vaidika Brahmans of the place clubbed together and made two entertainments; four came off in the houses of the laymen; and after that again the merchants made another in the house of a Brahman.'

'Did you ever go and pay your respects to the throne ?'

'Yes; two or three times. The throne is about as high as a man. It is completely covered with all sorts of figures and *salagrams*. The Swami always sits on a seat of silver filigree work, dressed in silk, and making *pugah* with saffron. I heard say, too, that the throne contains *stri-yantra*, and that even in his previous *asrama** the Swami was a most ardent student of the *stri-viaya*. Whether this be true or not I can't say; but, at all events, a fellow, who actually saw it happen, told me in confidence that even now the Swami conceals his face of a dark night and sallies out with one of his

* For note on this word see chapter vi., page 70.

people to perform his devotions to the first *stri* (woman) that he meets.* Besides what a disciple ran away with only the other day, there's still some two thousand rupees' worth of silver decorations about the throne ?'

'While in the place, did he take any steps to prevent the intermixture of various castes, or to propagate his religion ?'

'No, nothing of the kind; but there was one capital thing he did. In that town there lives a wealthy young widow. Some of the chief men of the village *panchiat*, or local court, on some plea or other, excommunicated her from caste. But when she afterwards made a feast in honour of Jagannahda, some Brahmans who were greedy of gain partook of the good cheer. So it happened that they split into two parties—all who went to the dinner on the one side, and all who didn't go on the other. It is money that makes the mare go, the world over; and the widow was wily enough to perform a number of religious vows—that of offering a *lac* of lighted lamps, among others—and to feast the Brahmans now and then; so the portion of the *panchiat* that took her part gradually grew so powerful, that the very ones who at first pronounced her sentence of excomunication now stand expelled themselves. Then the Swami came along and reconciled the two parties, got personally some two hundred rupees out of the widow, and had her hair shaved. The day after the grand hair-cutting ceremony, he had an entertainment at her house, when he first took the *hastoduka* † himself, and then had

---

* *Stri* or *sekti*, the Female Principle or Durga—personified energy in the form of a goddess. *Stri-vidya*, the general knowledge of this principle, its worship and use. *Stri-yantra*, a talismanic plate endowing the possessor with the power of using this energy. The final allusion to *stri* (woman) is a pun upon the technical use of the word, such priests being bound to celibacy.

† When Brahmins sit down to their meal, the host or hostess pours into the hand of each guest the *hastodaka*, or 'hand-water,' with the grace, 'May this be to you the elixir of life.' To receive this water the right hand is held palm upward, the forefinger elevated, and the thumb laid along inside it. The chief guest first sips the water, after which all the others follow suit.

it served to all the Brahmans, and restored her to caste from that very day.

'Where did this Swami reside during his former *asrama* ?'

'He lived at Mungonda-agrahara. He has four sons. 'Twas only a little while after he entered this *asrama* that he paid off the old debts upon his lands, got his four sons married, and presented each of his daughters-in-law with jewelry worth two hundred rupees. His name is now Sri Chidananda Sankarabharati-swami, so they say.'

At this stage of the conversation they reached the Rajah's palace. The Maharajah had already arrived, and was seated upon his throne.

After reading and disposing of the petitions which his chief minister presented for his consideration, he ordered the thieves who had been brought from Pitapuram to be placed before him. Just then Rajasekhara, Subrahmanya, and Nrusimhaswami entered the court and took their seats in a place befitting their station. The Royal constables then conducted the burglars into their lord's presence, and took up a position beside them with drawn swords. The Rajah ran his eyes over the assembly and asked : 'Where are the persons who apprehended these thieves ?' Subrahmanya at once rose in his place and respectfully replied that he was the person. His Highness immediately turned his gaze upon Rajasekhara and asked : 'Is this not your son ?' 'If it please your Highness,' replied Rajasekhara. 'And who,' again asked the Rajah, 'is he at your left ?' Rajasekhara now rose and, with joined hands, related at length how that he was his son-in-law; how an ill-wisher had, while he was in Benares, brought them a groundless report of his death ; and how, after they had all gone off and left Rukmini, while she was unconscious from a blow inflicted by the highway robbers, she had revived, and afterwards happening to be in the village to which Sita was taken, returned to them in man's dress. The Maharajah manifested his deep interest in the remarkable narrative by repeatedly shaking his head; and, after a moment's silence, turned towards the prisoners. 'What,' he demanded, 'have you got to say for yourselves?'

'What remains for us to say,' replied Niladri-rajah, 'in the worshipful presence of a ruler who is cognizant of all things? We will not profess ourselves to be innocent. Your Highness is ever actuated by the most perfect kindness of heart, and we humbly crave that your indulgence may be extended towards us.'

'What is your native country? Where have you lived since your boyhood? And what is your history?'

'My history is a most remarkable one, I confess I should be ashamed to relate it; but since a person of so exalted a rank desires to hear my story, I will tell it frankly. Whenever I am unemployed my conscience brings to my recollection the many evil deeds I have committed in the past, and torments me in a thousand ways. At night it will not let me sleep. Even in my dreams I start up in a fright thinking the royal constables are carrying me off to punish me for the terrible crimes I have committed. Besides this, old age is now upon me, and I cannot live long. Whenever I think of this my body quakes through fear of the emissaries of Satan. The ancients say that those who receive chastisement from the king are not punished by the devil. So I desire you to punish me for my sins in order that I may enjoy happiness hereafter.'

'Very good. Granted that your history is as remarkable as you represent it to be, let us hear it at greater length. All present here will be very glad to listen.'

'My native place is Kalahasti. Although my parents were not very rich, they belonged to a most respectable branch of the Sudra caste. As I was their only son I was bred with great indulgence. No matter what I said I wanted, they immediately gave it me. When I was five years of age however, they sent me to school, presenting the master with a web of girdle-cloth at the same time. This master had been unable to get a living in any other way, and had entered the profession of corpse-carrying; when growing old, he at last came to our village and opened a school as a means of subsistence, although he had never learned to read when young. Not a single particle of instruction could he impart, but he made up for this unimportant defect by showering upon our unlucky backs a *lac* of blows for every letter in the alphabet. But he was very good to those who gave him money; and I used to make over to him half the money my parents allowed me for small feed, and so escaped the beatings, For this reason he became exceedingly fond of me and put me in charge of the school, telling my parents that he knew no boy possessed of such good sense as their son. And from my very childhood I certainly was a most clever and ingenious lad. Although by my ingenuity I never brought my father and mother even so much as a drilled cowrie's worth of gain, but simply loss, yet they, good souls, rejoiced to think me smart. I used to employ my whole stock of cleverness solely in deceiving others. Had I devoted half as much care to the learning of some trade as I did to learning the art of roguery, how rich I might have been by this time! But let that go. After securing the management of the school I used to threaten the children that I would report them to the master and have them beaten, and in this way possessed myself of their eatables as bribes not to tell. While things were moving on in this way, by my ill luck the master died. At that time a master was counted able in proportion as he beat excessively. An educated master had already established a school in our village, but as he was kind to the children and wouldn't undertake to beat them without some reason, people wouldn't send their children to him at all. But there was now no second master in the village, and so it unluckily became necessary to send all our children there. But I couldn't get off any of my former pranks at all on this new master. About that time my father suddenly contracted heart disease and passed into the

other world. And as he breathed his last without any
intimation whatever as to where he had buried his
money, old Mother Misfortune came all the quicker and
took us under her wing. There was at that time studying in our school a young fellow, son of one of our rich
neighbours. He was excessively fond of study. I
struck up a friendship, gave him much of my confidence,
and made him my chum generally. Some, when they
repose confidence in anyone, are content to give their
heart along with it. I was a crafty chap and didn't
fall into this trap. Though I bestowed a thousand con-
fidences, in no case did I reveal my real thoughts, but
kept them carefully concealed. By this means I deceived him in many ways and obtained money again
and again. What jugglery there was in the matter, I
don't know; it mattered not how many frauds I practised upon him to obtain money, I was still poor and he
rich. In proportion as he advanced in his education I
became skilled in gaming. I abandoned study for the
companionship of wicked associates, and began to bet
and gamble. So ensnared by this vice did I become
that I even carried off things from the house by theft
or violence, and disposed of them to the master of the
game. But all this time I did not forget my obliga-
tions to my neighbour's son. In this way I passed my
sixteenth year. My friend now came of age and became master of a house of his own; and having a
relish for learning, he spent his whole time in scholarly
pursuits. One day I went to him and told him my
circumstances—how my father had been a trader, and I
was desirous of engaging in trade as well—and begged
him to assist me by advancing some money as capital.
Replying that he himself would be my partner, he
handed me two hundred rupees, binding me at the same
time by a compact that I was to do the work, that he
should take no interest, and that each should have half
the profits. Miserably small as our profits were, I did
all the work, and so I soon began to quarrel with my
friend for a larger share of the gains. Kings, though

they have kingdoms to enjoy, fight with one another
and die; while *byragis* who possess nothing more than
a mere clout are content to live without quarrelling.
One who is satisfied with what God has given him will
have few troubles; but if once he become dissatisfied
and possessed by the devil of desire, his troubles know
no end. But my friend was a very fine fellow and
generous to a fault. One day he called me in and said:
 '" As you have been a trader from the very first,
you're naturally fond of money. I, on the other hand,
am fond only of this wealth of learning. Provided you
are not hard up for creature comforts, the mere possession of money delights you. But as far as I am concerned, it is sufficient if I live respectably. So do you
take these two hundred rupees," said he, making over to
me the money he had advanced. Overjoyed that I had
gotten it into my own hands, I shut up shop and began
to gamble day and night with greater assiduity than
ever, and in a few months had squandered everything
and become a beggar. Then I repented of my rashness.
I hadn't even enough to eat. So one day I went to my
friend in patched clothes and praised his former kindness in various ways, and told him unreservedly the
sad plight I was in. When he learned my condition he
was deeply grieved; but knowing that if I had money
in hand I would waste it, he wrote a note to a friend
and sent me off with it. As soon as I had delivered
the letter he assigned me a position on a salary of ten
rupees per month and told me to come back at noon.
By the time I had been a couple of months at that
business it became intolerable. And then because I
used to make the articles that stuck to me when I was
alone vanish by sleight of hand, my master exploded
right and left and abused me terribly. Besides this, it
didn't suit my disposition to be subordinate and always
to do just as I was told. I have naturally a desire to
be like a Maharajah. So I left that work and came
home and sat with one leg over the other and lived
happily as long as I could raise a loan by con-

tinually borrowing from all who would trust me. While thus living unemployed I would never follow the kind advice of others, but I was exceedingly diligent in asking such advice, and in this way learned a lot of moral axioms. I considered that even though my ethics were never of any use to myself, they might at least benefit others. In this way I got the name of being a great man, and began to grow rich by giving apt counsel to fools. But you see, my own walk was not straight; and one day along came a man of real piety and asked me if, while I was preaching so much morality, my own conduct was upright. "Of course," replied I as became the occasion; "it is only because morality is of no use to me that I abandon it to you. If it benefited me in the least, do you think I'd allow a single particle of it to escape my hold?" I concluded, however, that I could do no further business in my native place; so I left hastily with the intention of going to foreign parts. Once off, I rested for a day only in each village, did not sleep in the village in which I ate my meals, and travelled incessantly. One day just outside a village I saw a large flock of goats, and wondering how the shepherd could care for so many, out of sheer pity for him I put a couple of kids on my shoulder and walked off, on the principle that to lighten his burden but a little was still to lighten it some. Seeing me carry off her kids the mother came running after me bleating. I thought it would be a sin for the mother to leave the children, so I drove her along too. The shepherd saw how matters stood and came running after me shouting, "Stop thief!" Up to that moment I had been afraid I would be very late in reaching the next village; but spurred on by his shouts I got there in a twinkling, and turned and looked back, pleased with my success. He had been unable to overtake my pace, and fearing that some one would carry off the remaining goats, had just at that moment turned about. In a neighbouring village I sold the mother and kids and retained the money for my travelling expenses. A few days later I reached Kondavid, where I turned *yogi*. Announcing that I had in my possession a *Seetarama-yantra** and that all who beheld it would become enormously wealthy, I placed a stone image in my room and began to show it *sub rosa* at the rate of a penny a head. No matter how vile an object be, 'twill increase immensely in respectability by keeping it concealed. Just as the vulgar herd give alms to the priests for the sake of seeing for themselves what the idols in the temples at the sacred shrines are like, so all the people were fetching me presents, and coming and going in crowds to see that stone image! Once seen, everybody began to regard it with contempt as only an ordinary stone such as you can see in the street, just as they do those ugly idols carved by awkward workmen. It is an undeniable fact that had I shown in the street for a single day the stone I placed in the house and exhibited as a *Seetarama-yantra*, the next day not one would have had the slightest desire to look at it. During the time I passed as a *yogi* I attained great celebrity both in magic and in witchcraft. Everybody boasted of my skill. Even my incantations were listened to by all with as much eagerness as were the tales of the demons I undertook to exorcise. But as the former, like the latter, served only the more to increase the fears of those who heard them, the villagers began to be alarmed as to what enchantment I might practise.

'While I was making money and living happily by this trick I fell sick, and although formerly I had preached up to any number of people that death was simply union with God, and that they should rejoice to attain to it, I now began to fear that I was going to die. Call any *yogi* you please, and ask him if he has any fear of death, and he will reply without hesitation that he has not; but wait until he gets a little sick—you may then see by his conduct that he is even a greater coward than the fools about him. While I was thus

---

* A talismanic image.

palming myself off as a *yogi*, it mattered not what *yogi* was praised in my hearing, I'd belittle him for a nobody. Is it not a rule that when the worthy are desirous of gaining a good name the unworthy take every pains to destroy their reputation and make it as mean as their own?

'As I have related, I assumed many disguises, and at last became a *byragi*, when I took these two on as disciples, entered Dhavalesvaram under the name of Chidananda-yogi, fooled even Rajasekhara here with my promises of gold, and carried off these jewels that have just now been brought to your Highness. After leaving there I shaved off my beard and moustache and came to Pitapuram as Niladri-rajah, where, with the help of these fellows, I walked off with the money in the Rajah's treasury. My wonderful exploits in these two places, as well as my conduct, Rajasekhara and his son can well relate; and besides, it is unseemly to praise oneself; so with this I shall stop.'

After hearing this story the Maharajah reflected a moment and turned towards Padmanabhudu and said: 'As you seem now to have come to your senses, and repented of your misdeeds, we have decided to imprison you for but one year.' He then wrote an order to the gaoler and despatched the prisoner to Samalkot in the custody of constables. He next bade his chief minister send off at once the money belonging to the Rajah of Pitapuram; and, after expressing his high appreciation of Subrahmanya's conduct in the detection of the burglars, turned to Rajasekhara and addressed him thus:

'Though it has been your lot to undergo so many trials in the past, you have survived all your misfortunes, and have now attained to a position such that you may live happily. For this reason I am going to give you some friendly counsel. You will give your full attention to my remarks. To rise after a fall is greatness, but there is nothing great, believe me, in never falling at all. Do you keep this truth in mind and cease to worry about trials which are past for ever.

Hereafter do not allow yourself to be puffed up by the flatteries of others. Do not spend more money than your income affords. It is possible for members of the same family to be most affectionate in their behaviour one toward another in the presence of outsiders, and to be deadly enemies the moment they reach home. So you must look after your family with such care that no defect of this kind shall exist in it. The best expedient for overcoming ill-will is undoubtedly the exercise of meekness. If we desire to pay off a grudge against anyone, and feel ourselves unable to do it, we should suppress our anger at least until we become wealthy. And even when we possess the power to gratify our thirst for revenge, if we can forgive the injury, even our enemies will become the wiser and better for our example. The toad that undertakes to bite will meet with just about as much success as will the poor man who undertakes to get the upperhand of a wealthy one. Who cares for anger that ends in empty threats? Not only are we unable to achieve our object by such anger, but (and this is more important) we are sure to lose by it. It was because you flew into a rage at Sobhanadrirajah, was it not, that you were incarcerated? So do you never again get angry with those who are of higher rank than yourself. There are some senseless persons who would persuade one that there is no time like the past, and who would make one unhappy by imputing his faults to the age in which he lives. But on mature reflection it seems to me that the present age is in all respects a better one than the past. Merit and demerit exist in men's conduct, and not in the age that produces them. Do not, therefore, blame the times for your mistakes, but use your best endeavours to rectify your own conduct. If you have sufficient means to enable you to live with respectability, never worry because you have not more. Listen while I relate to you an ancient fable illustrative of this truth. Once upon a time a certain rich man was passing along the street decorated profusely with golden jewelry studded with precious stones. A beggar who happened to catch sight of him followed behind gazing upon the jewels, and saluting humbly again and again. Observing his peculiar conduct the rich man exclaimed : " What, I haven't given you any of my jewels, have I ? Why do you do that ?" " I do not want your jewels," replied the beggar, " but you allowed me to look at them, and for that reason I am saluting you. Even you can get no other good from these jewels than the pleasure of looking at them ; and besides, how much pains are you put to to guard them from accident. Now, it is for the very reason that I have no such trouble that I have so much happiness. That is the difference between you and me, in a nutshell." So, although I am able to make you very rich, I shall not, for the reasons I have just mentioned ; but shall content myself with merely redeeming your estates and restoring them to you. May you rest content with them and spend the remainder of your days in peace.'

Having administered this sound advice the Maharajah asked Rajasekhara whether he had any wish he desired to make known. Rajasekhara in reply eulogised the noble character of his lord, recounted the great kindness he had done his family, and begged him to release from imprisonment Manchirajah Papayya, who had rendered him such signal assistance in writing and sending the petition, and in many other ways, while in prison. Commending highly this exhibition of good feeling toward a whilom enemy who had done him injury, the Rajah at once despatched an order for the prisoner's release, and, having brought the proceedings to a close in due form, retired to his chamber. Thereupon Rajasekhara and the others present left the court and proceeded to their homes.

CHAPTER XV.

Rajasekhara returns to his Native Place—Subrahmanya's Marriage—Marriage of Sita—Rajasekhara, made wise by trials endured, passes the rest of his days in peace.

In accordance with the Rajah's command Rajasekhara came the next day to court, when the Maharajah Krishna Jagapati called one of his councillors and ordered a bag of rupees to be brought and placed before him. This money he then handed over to the councillor, bidding him take it to Dhavalesvram, and with it redeem Rajasekhara's house and lands, and restore them to him. He then turned to Rajasekhara and handed him four hundred rupees in addition to the amount he had already given. 'With this money,' said he, 'you are to conduct Subrahmanya and Sita's weddings. Never spend more than your income, and may you pass the remainder of your days in peace.' With these parting words the Rajah dismissed him.

When Rajasekhara returned to Bhimavaram after taking leave of the Maharajah he learned that someone, a relative, had come from Jaggampeta, and was waiting at the house. On hearing this he hurried on home, where he found an aged brahman seated upon the *pial*. On Rajasekhara asking him who he was, he replied that his family name was Bhavarajah, and that his own name was Suryanarayana. 'And are you not Rajasekhara?' he inquired.

'I am. On what business have you come?'

'A lad named Subbarayadu came to your house a little while ago. Where is he now?'

'So far as I know no lad of that name has come here.'

'When the kidnappers carried off your daughter he brought her back here from our village. He had made a vow to Venkatesvara and grown his hair long. He was a very handsome lad. He told us that he was going to your house along with some Rajah or other. When little, he got his education from you, I think.'

'What business have you with him?'

'He stayed at our place for some time. We were pleased with his ability and good looks, and as I have no male issue we decided to give him my daughter in marriage and keep him with us.'

Rajasekhara now related to his visitor the story of Rukmini's assuming male attire under the name Subbarayadu, and the other wonderful events connected with their past history, and promised to marry the old Brahman's little girl to his son Subrahmanya. At this Suryanarayana was as delighted as a beggar who has found a magnificent fortune; and, taking an immediate leave of Rajasekhara, he came back the next day, bringing his wife and daughter along with him. On the same day Rajasekhara had bandies brought and set out in the cool of the evening for Rajahmundry, which place he reached in two or three days in company with his new friend Suryanarayana. After spending a couple of days there at Ramamurti's house he gathered together the brass utensils he had placed in his safe keeping, took his cousin and his family also along to the wedding, and at length reached Dhavalesvaram in safety.

The Maharajah's councillor who had come down from Peddapuram now released and made over to Rajasekhara his lands and house, and was about to return to his master, when Rajasekhara began to dissuade him with such persistency that he consented to remain until the weddings of his host's son and daughter came off.

No sooner was it known that Rajasekhara had returned to the place rich and redeemed his lands, than all the old friends who had kept out of sight when poverty fastened upon him, began to bestir themselves. A whole host of sycophants, who before would not vouchsafe a reply even when addressed, now began to circumambulate the house a half dozen times a day. The menial herd who formerly were never to be found when most wanted, now crowded the doorway from morning to night, without so much as a hint of cooly or

13

wages. Both Ramasastri and the astrologer called, and, as usual, exhibited their learned ability in flattering our hero to his face—only with twice as much skill as before. But Rajasekhara had already had a taste of their art; and these worthies discovered in him but few traces of that liberality and appreciativeness which had of old given them returns at the rate of a *lac* for each word they uttered. The astrologer, supposing that possibly it was he with whom Rajasekhara was angry, and desiring to be reinstated in his good graces, brought over, with the aid of a cooly, the box of jewelry belonging to Damodarayya, which had been concealed in his house, and delivered it to Rajasekhara. Besides this, he began to praise Rajasekhara in the hearing of relatives and friends who would, he knew, carry his words to the right ears. The very mouth that had declared that he had never seen so bad a horoscope as Subrahmanya's, now that that critical period of the boy's existence was past, fell to lauding it as the most incomparable horoscope in the world. Hearing this, the parties who, in Rajasekhara's poverty, had refused to give their child, now began to revolve about Rajasekhara, and to pester him by all means to marry their daughters to Subrahmanya, even offering to give a dowry of four hundred rupees into the bargain. Though these people were wealthy and in the habit of giving their sons-in-law donations of money and other articles, Rajasekhara would none of their girls, but resolved to unite his son in marriage with Mahalaksmi, the daughter of Suryanarayana.

So, with due regard to the auspiciousness of the time, Rajasekhara made a wedding for his son. Though there were those who averred that a wedding without music and dancing could not be lucky, he paid no heed to their remarks; and considering that at a time so well calculated to teach conjugal fidelity they should have nothing to do with dancers, he spent but little for the songs of dancing women, but had some of the finest singers of the place render a number of religious hymns in their most pleasing manner. On the third day, when the time for distributing the gifts came, instead of presenting them to unworthy persons, he bestowed this honour, so far as he was able, upon a few worthy people and *pandits* only ; and to those people who remonstrated with him that, if he did not give presents to all the Brahmans present, they would feel very mean, he replied that it was certainly better to hang one's head during the five days of the wedding and to hold it high afterwards, than to carry it high for a few days and then, the prey of debt, to hang it for ever in shame ; and managed the whole affair precisely in accordance with his own wishes. On the ground that it was simply a waste of money to fill up the street with a great *pandal* and open a *choultry* for the occasion, he invited and made welcome to dinner only relatives and friends. By conducting the wedding in this way, the expense was actually less than he had at first reckoned ; so he took the remainder of the money and had some jewels made for his daughter-in-law.

Three days after the son's wedding came to an end, Rajasekhara bestowed Sita's hand upon his nephew Sankarayya. This second wedding was in all respects exactly similar to that which had just preceded it. On both of these occasions the promiscuous and surreptitious snatching of plates from one another at dinner, stupid horse-play, and the indecent practice of raising pandemonium at pleasure, without distinction of sex, while sprinkling odiferous powder and scarlet water after the final ceremony, were abandoned. Those who were deprived of the power to earn a living, by such bodily defects as lameness and blindness ; poor people who had fallen into their wretched condition through no fault of their own, but by the act of God ; *pandits* who were upright in conduct and versed in all branches of learning ; and the confessedly pious : these only were honoured with gifts of money.

* *Pandal*, a light shed of open bamboos covered with palmira-leaves. Here dinner is served to all of the same caste who care to partake of it.

After these two events had passed off in due form, the councillor who had come down from Peddapuram one day approached Rajasekhara and begged that he might be excused, as he had to take his departure without delay.

'Since you yielded to my entreaty and remained these past ten days, you must please me by staying for the *finale* as well before you think of leaving.'

'You really must excuse me and let me go at once. A letter has just now reached me, which states that Acharya-swami, who had come to our village before we set out for this place, has written a bull of excommunication, or something of that sort, against my nephew, on the plea that when he sent in his pastoral letter, my nephew, instead of immediately forking out the rupees, treated the matter with indifference; that for the past three days no one will cross his threshold, and that even now neither will the barber come to shave him nor the washerman to wash the clothes. If his Reverence the Swami excommunicates, the neighbours will neither give fire nor allow one to draw water from their wells.'

'Why, the swamis should abandon all such passions as avarice and desire for revenge, and be the meekest of the meek. Do they inflict such severe punishment for so small a fault?'

'So far as the mere name goes you may call him a *Swami*; but the truth is, he's got the worst temper in the world. What you see now is nothing at all. Why, only last year this very *swami* while in Chicaole cracked a joke of some kind with the wife of the master of a house where he was being entertained, and the man happening to overhear it said nothing, through fear that if he reproved a priest he would be fined, but at the close of the feast merely declined to give a contribution; when what do you think the *swami* did?—expelled him for three months and then took fifty rupees from the poor fellow and made him undergo penance before he would receive him into caste again. Unless I go at once and induce my nephew to beg forgiveness on condition of paying a fine, the thing will not be hushed up. So do not force me to stay longer, but send me on my way this very day.'

'When you represent matters in this light, it certainly would be wrong to detain you longer,' replied Rajasekhara, as he tied about him some new cloths. So, after doing him every honour that lay in his power, and instructing him as to the messages he was to convey, with Rajasekhara's deepest gratitude, to the Maharajah, he gave his guest leave. Shortly afterwards the numerous guests who had come in for the wedding returned to their respective homes.

A few days after hearing that Rajasekhara had returned to the place rich, Narayanamurti called one day and informed Rajasekhara as a secret that he and Damodarayya had been bosom friends, that at the time of Damodarayya's death the villagers, for no other reason than that he was the dead man's friend, had stolen all his household stuff, and that he was now hard pressed even for food and clothing, and—would not Rajasekhara render him a little assistance?

'It is not possible for me,' replied Rajasekhara, ' to show kindness to such an ingrate and violator of friendship as you are. It mattered not how much good I did you, when I got into difficulties and craved your assistance you refused it and turned your back upon me even though able to help. Though Damodarayya was your bosom friend you thought to make away with the box which he committed to your care, instead of handing it over to the son of your dead friend.

'It was the astrologer himself who first suggested to me that I should hide the box in his house, and who hinted that it would be a very easy matter to make away with it. After I had delivered the cash box to him he quarrelled with me for a half share of the contents, and when I, unwilling to see a friend's money come into possession of a stranger, refused to agree to his proposal, he brought the box to you for the sake of your good will.'

'Even though the astrologer did urge you to it, you are the guilty party, and in no way can you show yourself to be innocent. It is by your own premeditated crime that this misfortune has come upon you, and there is no way out of it but for you to enjoy the fruit of your folly.'

With these biting words Rajasekhara sent him about his business without rendering him a single anna's assistance.

From that time onward Rajasekhara, having gained dear experience from the conduct of the astrologer and others of that ilk, took good care never to allow himself to be puffed up by empty adulations, nor to squander his money, and steadily refused to believe anyone his friend who approached him with oily words. Through the base trick which the *yogi* had practised upon him he was convinced that all of that name were at the best only gluttons. He became, too, a firm disbeliever in *mantras* and alchemy, with all kindred arts. As for the demons with which Rukmini had but a short time before been possessed, as well as witch-doctoring, divination, and similar impostures—since everybody's belief in such deceptions had evaporated, such a thing as demoniacal possession, or symptoms of enchantment, or divine inspiration, was never afterwards known in the family. From the circumstance that the horoscopes of the members of his family, as well as the numerous lucky times determined for various events, invariably turned out in a manner directly opposite to that prognosticated, both Rajasekhara and his descendants became disbelievers in astrology as well. On account of the trials he had undergone through debts contracted for gratuities at Rukmini's wedding, Rajasekhara determined never again to go in debt. From that time onward he wasted no money on useless show, but continued most moderate in all his expenditure ; and, content with what God had granted him, bestowed upon the poor alms of what he possessed. Preserving truth and kindheartedness inviolate even in his dreams—

treasuring ever in his heart the golden maxim that
'Virtue is victory'—and departing not the length of a
fly's foot from the path of righteousness, he conducted
himself honestly in the sight of all men, gained the
reputation in the land of being a good man, and spent
the rest of his days in affluence and happiness, surrounded by numerous grandsons and granddaughters.
While his father was yet alive Subrahmanya attained to
a lucrative position in the Pitapuram Court, finally
became *mantri*,* and won a name unrivalled for
statesmanship and justice. The two sons-in-law obtained
employment in the court of the Maharajah of Peddapuram, and gradually rose to eminence and great
celebrity. Besides these particular members of Rajasekhara's family, many of his numerous host of relatives,
too, who by dishonest practices had enjoyed the
pleasures of sin for a season, learned by Rajasekhara's
upright walk that honesty is the only source of enduring
good, and finally entered the path he trod so un-
erringly.

Beholding with his own eyes that same astrologer's
daughter, who when a girl was said to be haunted by
her dead husband, now a woman grown, elope (taking
with her all she could lay hands upon in the house)
with another woman's living husband, go to the bad,
and at last take to walking the streets of the town
before her father's very eyes—beholding the miseries
endured by unfortunate women who had lost their
husbands in their early youth—beholding such women,
unable to withstand the uncontrollable promptings of
desire, become entangled in the net of libertines and
ruin of both body and soul—and beholding others, fearful of the anathemas of their caste, surrender themselves secretly to such horrible crimes as infanticide
and abortion—Rajasekhara's heart melted with pity,
and he set himself to work with the determination to
make a strenuous effort to alleviate the crying misery
of these wretched child-widows. But, unable to con-

* *I.e.*, Prime Minister.

vert to his views the consummately ignorant people, and *pandits* who were really fools through inspiration of the demon of custom, Rajasekhara, unsuccessful in his noble efforts, shortly departed to a better world. Although two hundred years have now passed away since Rajasekhara departed this life, the descendants of those whose condition was ameliorated through his noble efforts still eulogize his sterling worth. Rajasekhara's descendants themselves have spread over the whole country, and have, in many places, attained to great eminence.

THE END.

www.ingramcontent.com/pod-product-compliance
Lightning Source LLC
Chambersburg PA
CBHW031818220426
43662CB00007B/697